BORN BOUNDLESS

REALIZING YOUR IDENTITY AND POWER TO SOAR

ISBN: 13:978-0-6921-6791-5

ISBN: 10:0-6921-6791-9

BORN BOUNDLESS

Dedication
My deepest appreciation and gratitude

I would like to dedicate *Born Boundless* to the will and the work of the Holy Spirit who has given me the grace needed to persevere even during difficult times. It took the Holy Spirits continuous prompting that I finally realized – Now! Is the time.

I am grateful for spiritual leaders that covered me through prayer and supplication as I embarked upon this new journey. Special thanks to Chief Apostle and Senior Pastor Jacque McCollough at Manna from Heaven Ministries, Intl. for their spiritual insight and prophetic utterance which helped me to birth this book.

My dear sister, Laura Murph who has always been so supportive and always eagerly awaiting in confident expectation the next move of God. Thanks for the long hours spent together, long phone calls that lasted sometimes more than two hours at a time. Thanks for allowing me to ramble on and on, the quiet times of listening and tears wept. Not only are you my sister, but I call you "Friend".

I love you, Sister Laura…

Born

: Brought into life by birth. Being in specified circumstances from birth; having special natural abilities or character from birth

Boundless

: Having no boundaries; vast possibilities, endless

TABLE OF CONTENT

INTRODUCTION

My Life. My Journey. My Story.

Born Boundless was birthed out of my quiet time with the Lord a couple of years ago. This book is an affirmation of who you really are. It's not about who you will be some day in the distant future, or who you might be if you work harder, but who you are today. God knows your end from your beginning, so he looks at your ending and he declares that you are boundless. You can do, be or have anything you set your mind to without limitation. I heard this from my mom as a child because she instilled in each of us that we could be whatever we wanted to be, but I never knew how to attain it. Anyone who knows me, know that I am a communicator and very analytical. When I was young, I use to hear people say "It is not good to be analytical". My mother had to constantly remind me to stop asking so many questions. I never understood why, so I never gave it much thought until a few years ago. I found myself writing things down in a journal, always looking for answers to things that no one could explain. As I grew older and began to mature in the things of God, the Holy Spirit began to give me revelation to uncovered mysteries and provided me with the key that unlocked my future. I know now that even being analytical as a child, I was desperately searching and seeking to know my identity. God has put a longing in our hearts to know him, to seek his purpose and will for our lives. It is not by chance nor error that your desire to seek after things is there, but you are seeking the wrong things. Many of the things that you are seeking are leading you further and further from his presence. Since my discovery, I have never discarded my analytical ability to closely examine, inspect, investigate or dissect anything to reach sound judgement in a matter which by the way got me to where I am today.

One morning during my devotional reading, I remember my scripture reading was in John 8:36 NIV when Jesus was addressing the Pharisees and letting them know that *"So if the Son sets you free, you will be free indeed"*. I pondered on that for a while and after reading the scripture I sat back and the Holy Spirit took me on a spiritual journey, and I began to look at my life, my family, people on the job who were Christians and people in the church. I asked the Holy Spirit a question, "If we are sons and daughters and Jesus came to set us free – Why are we still bound?" I could not rap my mind around this spiritual truth because I did not feel free. Why does it feel like I am stuck, like I can't go any further? Why do I feel like there are invisible perimeters that have been set up to define how far I can go? Why do I feel so defined by people? Why do I feel restricted to only work certain types of jobs which are leading me nowhere?

Why do I feel that going back to school is unattainable? Why do I feel hindered and limited by my own thinking? Why am I always reminded of past failures that always seem to haunt me? I would have good thoughts of where I wanted to go in life and what I needed to do to get there, but I always came up short. I never really saw myself doing it, although I rejoiced with those who did. Mediocrity or small thinking, is like a computer virus that had infiltrated my mind. I remember ten years ago I was working on my computer and I had received and email from an unknown source telling me my that the software on my computer has expired and that I needed to buy some new software. When I clicked on the icon to make the purchase, a virus was immediately downloaded to my computer and within a matter of seconds my computer crashed. I took my computer to several places to see if it could be restored. I could get it restored, but I was told that it would cost more to restore my old computer than it would be to just put it in the trash and buy a new one. The computer was already about five years old and they wanted to charge me over a thousand dollars to restore it. The guy at Best Buy store, said "we have some brand-new computers on the shelf for about three hundred dollars". I did not want a new computer, everything I owned was on that computer, my pictures, video's, copies of letters, resume's, things that I had scanned. That's how your mind is when it is not renewed, like a computer that has been infected by a virus. They make antivirus software that you can download to protect and safeguard your computer against viruses and malware. That's what the word of God does once it is downloaded. It will destroy and remove anything from your spiritual hard drive that have been planted by the enemy making sure there are no threats or viruses and ensure your system is running at optimal speed.

Your own mind is keeping you in bondage and we have all been down that road before and you may even be there now. You may be doing all the right things but getting nowhere. In a still quiet voice, The Holy Spirit revealed to me that it was all a lie and that those were just whispers from the enemy to keep my feet planted on the ground. We live in a fallen world and people are more apt

Lies are a Deception the Enemy

You belong to your father, the devil, and you want to carry out your father's desire. He was a murder from the beginning, not holding the truth, for there is no truth in him. When he lies, he speaks his native language, for he is a liar and the father of lies.

John 8:44-45 NIV

to consume themselves with dead things. Things that are not growing or producing good things are considered dead. We hear so much negativity rather than positive, but have you noticed that positive thinking and positive words are not automatic, but you must consciously choose them? As the Holy Spirit began to minister to me, it was like a loving parent to a child; He said "You were born boundless".

As I began to weep, he shared with me how it was not the original intent of the father that any of his children should have to suffer, experience loss, death, be in bondage, or have failing health issues.   In other words, being boundless was not something that momma could teach me, and I cannot learn it in school. Some things in your life are only revealed to you by the Holy Spirit because they are spiritual. Until you catch the revelation of what the Holy Spirit is speaking to you, you will never be able to soar, you will always be weighed down with the cares of this world. This is the same message that Jesus was conveying to the disciples when he was inquiring with them and he asked them a question. God's vision for your life may be greater than your vision, but if you agree with him, you will be able to see your destiny through his eyes. He will bear you up on eagle's wings and enable you to get to the place that her has ordained just for you. Your vision should be greater than where you are today because God is not through with you yet! Don't ever stop dreaming or striving to get to the place that God has for you.

There are a lot of people "trying to find themselves" which is a conflict in the mind that causes confusion about your personality. Just be who you are. Jesus told the disciples "you are the salt of the earth" There is no struggle in being yourself. The struggle comes from trying to be someone else or something that God did not call you to be.

You are the salt of the earth, but if the salt loses it saltiness, how can it be made salty again? It is no longer good for anything, except to be thrown out and trampled by men. (Mathew 5:13 NIV)

CHAPTER ONE
Mistaken Identity

We are all different although there are some similarities. There is something unique about you that sets you apart and it cannot be duplicated. You were created as a Single individual, your character, personality, nature, humor, peculiarity and your nonconformity make you different. Embrace your uniqueness and do not allow others to conform you to their accepted patterns, thoughts or actions. That is what the enemy is after, he is not after your car or your house, but it's your identity.

You can hear so much prosperity preaching and you obtain material wealth and now you are working harder to maintain material things while losing your salvation. Because if we are not careful it will lead to covertness, pride, idolatry, jealousy and envy. There is nothing wrong with material things if things are not worshiped and they are kept in their proper places. If the enemy can get you to think that you are not who God says you are, then you will have a twisted, warped or perverted view of self. A distorted view of self can lead to self-mutilation or cutting yourself, anorexia, and even thoughts of suicide. Whenever Gods view of you and your view of yourself does not align themselves, you will always live a defeated life and most people suffer in silence. I decree and declare that by the anointing and the power that rest upon my life, in the name of Jesus that every chain be broken and every yoke be destroyed. Be set free! In the name of Jesus.

CRAWSD

For you created my inmost being; you knit me together in my mother's womb. I praise you because I am fearfully and wonderfully made; your works are wonderful, I know that full well. (Psalm 139:13-14 NIV)

CRAWSD

Who do you say I am?

People are so inquisitive and are always talking about something. Most people will strike up a conversation with a stranger about the weather, news highlights, sports or something that they have heard. Everybody has something to say, and it was the same way in Jesus's' day. Whenever a person walks into a room of unfamiliar faces, the first thing most people ask is "who is that?" When Jesus ministry started, it was a public ministry and he was always talking about the kingdom. Jesus used parables to give them an earthly story about a spiritual kingdom. That's what I love most about his teaching because he never came to promote himself, but the kingdom. He spoke to doctors, lawyers, tax collectors, fisherman, prostitutes, educated and uneducated in a way that they could understand. The way Jesus taught back then is a little different than the time we live in. You hear less and less about the kingdom and holiness, but more and more about "the church". The way we view the "church" today is not the same way Jesus viewed the church because the church he was speaking about was spiritual. The church is not a building where people meet once a week although they did go to the temple as a meeting place to be taught.

A spiritual church is collective a body of believers that were separated from the world living a life of holiness. It is not a self-absorbed life of material gain. Back then, it was all about advancing the kingdom – nothing else mattered. The Pharisees, Sadducees, and Scribes were teaching from the first five books of Moses known as the Torah, which is the book of the law. They had not heard of such a kingdom that Jesus was talking about. They were waiting in great expectation that the Kingly Messiah would come and set up a natural kingdom on earth and to save them from the Roman dictatorship. When this did not happen, they thought that Jesus was preaching a new kind of doctrine and it made a lot of people angry because most of the people were so religious. They had been doing things a certain way for so long that when Jesus came, his teaching began tearing down the walls of traditions. It was painful for those stuck in traditions so, of course people were trying to figure out three things about Jesus. Who is he, were did he come from and by what authority do you do these things (miracles). Because Jesus knew the intent of their hearts, the scripture tells us that Jesus took his disciples to another place called Caesarea Philippi which was away from the religious leaders. Jesus inquired with his disciples and asked a very important question, one that will change history forever! (HIS- STORY).

This same question is also important and applies to you, so as you began to read this book I pray that you will allow the Holy Spirit to locate you on his spiritual radar. Until you can answer the question with all sincerity and conviction of heart – it will be virtually impossible for you to be totally free and go on to do greater works. I can image for a moment, time standing still as Jesus began to question his disciples. I remind you, if you have confessed your hope in Christ and are doing the work of the ministry, you are also a disciple. Jesus wanted his disciples to tell him "who do they say, that the son of man is?" Even in the world in which we live, everybody have their own opinion about who Jesus is. Some say he is a healer, some say he is a lawyer, some say miracle worker and some say he is a good man. Some say he is a prophet, some say he is a teacher and some say........... I hope you understand my point, yes – "Some say", but what about you. What do you say

Then he asked them, "But who do you say I am?" Simon Peter answered, "You are the Messiah, the Son of the living God." Jesus replied, "You are blessed, Simon of John," because my father in heaven has revealed has revealed this to you. You did not learn this from any human being. Now I say to you that you are Peter (which means rock), and upon this rock I will build my church, and all the powers of hell will not conquer it. And I will give you the keys of the Kingdom of Heaven. Whatever you forbid on earth will be forbidden in heaven, and whatever you permit on earth will be permitted in heaven." (Matthew 16:15-19 NLT)

To tell others about Christ or lead someone to Christ, you would have to know Him and not just know about him from information gathered from a book. You must have an experience or encountered transformation by Him whom you testify of. You are called out, therefore to draw people to the father, you need to exhibit the characteristics of the father. It wasn't until Peter answered the question that Jesus revealed to Peter that he would go on to turn the world upside down. Jesus already knew what everybody else was saying about him, but he was not concerned with everybody else. The disciples were apart of Jesus inner circle, hand-picked, taught and trained by Jesus, so their confession about Jesus should be different than what everyone else is saying. Once you spend time with people you will quickly learn about their character because a man's character cannot be hidden. You may be able to conceal your intent from the natural eye, but it will be revealed in the spirit.

The disciples walked with him daily, they broke bread together, and traveled with him. Everything that Jesus did, he also taught his disciples to do. Did you catch what just happened in the passage? Look at the conversation between Jesus and Peter. Notice how Peter reveals to Jesus that he knows who Jesus is (You are the Christ). It wasn't until after Peter made this public confession that Jesus revealed to Simon son of John (You are Peter which means rock) Now, that is transference of power and authority! Jesus blessed him and gave him the keys to the kingdom. Keys are important and represent binding and loosing. Keys can give you entry into a place and they can also lock you out. Keys are like a password to your computer, you cannot get in without it. No one can log onto your computer unless they know the password or the four-digit pin code. Most bank accounts are secure with pin numbers when using the ATM machine. The church is built on the foundation of who Jesus is. The revelation revealed to Peter by the Father is what will be used to build the kingdom. Once you get the revelation, you will be "Boundless"- unstoppable, no longer frustrated with the cares of this life because in the end, you win! The gates of hell or the powers of hell will not conquer it. That means the enemy will not be able to overpower you, he will not dominate, defeat, or subdue you if you walk in obedience and revelation. Most Americans suffer from identity crisis which cause you to look outside of yourself looking for something to connect with or identify with because of the desperate need to be validated.

Some people search for years and still never find it, while some use forms of sex, drugs, alcohol and the quest to attain power and control to numb this longing in their hearts. We are rapidly losing the teenage population to suicide or homicide from bullying or peer pressure associated with being different. Most relationships are divided due to indifference and our inability to change people to be like us or the way we think they should be, look and act. God never gave man the ability to change anyone, it takes the power of the Holy Spirit to change the heart of man. Apostle Paul was trying to get the church at Corinth to understand this truth. I preach to my family all the time and have been for many years not.

I have expressed to them over and over that my goal is to teach them to Jesus and not teach them to me. I am not trying to make a name for myself. Don't try to be like me, just be like Jesus. That was the message Paul preached, "follow me as I follow Christ". My identity is in Christ and apart from him, I have no identity.

"You see, we don't go around preaching about ourselves. We preach that Jesus Christ is Lord, and we ourselves are the servants for Jesus sake. For God who said "Let there be light in the darkness," has made this light shine in our hearts so we could know the glory of God that is seen in the face of Jesus Christ." (2 Cor4:5- 6NLT)

For many years I tried to be what people wanted me to be, what they thought I should be and even what they thought I could be while at the time, losing the unique identity of who I was created to be. I too have suffered loss of a failed marriage which led to alcohol consumption, over usage of pain medication, depression and suicidal tendencies that lasted a few years after the loss of my mother to cancer.

I had so many low times in my life that I can remember not wanting to live. My first suicide attempt was when I was only fourteen years old. It is amazing how no one around me could pick up on this, they never even suspected that anything was wrong even when I would separate myself from them for months and go into isolation. I can talk about it today because I am free. It is a little saddening to think about the times that I felt unloved, unwanted, unappreciated, and invaluable to such a point, I did not want to live because the pain of living was just mentally overwhelming. The picture that the enemy had painted in my mind about me was so distorted that it is only by the Grace of God, I am still here. I never knew my life had purpose. No one had ever told me how much Jesus loves me. I did not know that he loves me so much that before I came to earth, God had already spoken my destiny and sang songs of deliverance over me. No one told me that God had already called my life into being in the heavens and he equipped me with everything I needed before I arrived. While in his hands, he affirmed everything that I would and could do on earth. Destiny is calling you! You were created by God for his good pleasure. There is a plan, and a call on your life that is much greater than You. It was only through spending time with him, that I came to know him.

We are wealthy when it comes to information. We have so many books, tapes, DVD, CD's, audio books, conferences, seminars, and social media live. The disciples had none of that, but they turned the world upside down with what they had – a relationship. Information is right at our fingertips and that is all it is "information". Just because I read a good book about you, does not mean that I know you. You can tell me your husband name, where you went to school, your favorite foods and how many children you have. That does not mean that I know you. That is great informational knowledge, but I only know about you. I have learned over the years if you do not have a real relationship with Jesus, it is just information which is religion.

What lies have the enemy been speaking to you, about you or someone else? False perception of self, started in the Garden of Eden when Eve had the conversation with the serpent. He convinced her that if she eats the fruit, she would be like God. She was already "like God" because the book of Genesis tells us that human beings were created in the likeness and image of God. It is easy to alter a person's mindset and even change their perception with just one word because words have power because they are living and active.

❦

John 7:27-29 NIV

But we know where this man is from; when the Christ comes, no one will know where he is from." Then Jesus, still teaching in the temple courts, cried out, "Yes, you know me, and you know where I am from. I am not here on my own, but he who sent me is true. You do not know him, but I know him because I am from him and he sent me."

❦

That can easily happen to you if you do not know who you are in Christ. Have you ever seen a person make their mind up about a matter, but the moment they share it with a friend, relative or neighbor they allow someone else's decision to influence them? Now they are confused and don't know what to do and then they go around asking everybody, what do you think about this?

I think to myself sometimes – how is that? That is why it is not always good to share your ideas with everyone. The enemy will talk you out of what God has said. Listen to what I am saying, no one can change your mind when it is a God idea. Did you catch what I just said? A "God idea" is different from a "Good idea". Joseph in the bible had the same problem with his brothers when he told them what God showed him in a dream. They left him in a pit to die and then sold him right into slavery. The enemy knows your future and he also knows his future, but he has nothing to lose. The enemy recognize the need to be identified with the creator.

The only difference is, he did not want to be like God, he wanted to be God. I hope you see there is a big difference. The highest calling of humanity is not to be a prophet or a pastor, it's not to be a wife or mother. All of those are good in their respected place, but it is humbling to say the highest call of all humanity is to be transformed into the likeness and image of Christ.

Then God said, "Let us make human beings in our own image, to be like us. They will reign over the fish in the sea, the birds in the sky, the livestock, and all the wild animals on the earth, and the small animals that scurry along the ground." So, God created human beings in his own image. In the image of God, he created them; male and female. (Genesis 1: 26-27 NLT)

By now you are probably wondering what the title "Born Boundless" has to do with what I am talking about. A lot, because the scripture not only says God created you in his likeness and image, but it also said that he gave you dominion to reign. When Adam and Eve lost their identity, they also lost their dominion. Who did they lose it to? you may be wondering. They gave it to the serpent in the garden. They were trying to tell him what God said, and he was discrediting their testimony just like society has a way of displaying images of what society want you to look like, how you should talk, what you should wear, what school to attend, what kind of car you should drive, what kind of house to buy. We are bombarded with messages by TV, radio, internet, books and social media. God does not want you to be confused about who you are, or what your purpose is in life. This was revelation to me once I grasped what he was saying to me through the scriptures. He wants you to turn to his word to find out who you are. His word is like a mirror which is his image starring back at you. The more you look in the mirror (Word) you will see him because Jesus is the word. He and his word are one. The glory that he project will be the glory that you project because you will see yourself through him. That is why it is so important that the Body of Christ know who they are which is manifested out of relationship. Your identity comes from him. The more the Holy Spirit reveals Jesus to you, the more like Him you will become. Everything God created, he spoke into being, but you and I was created by his hand. It is interesting to know that in the book of Genesis, God saw and God said. That is an important fact because He saw the earth was dark and void, and without form. He never said what it was, he only called it what he wanted it to be. You have the same ability to calls things that are not, as though they were. You can speak things into existence. If you look in Genesis chapter 2 verse 19 and 20 it tells us how God brought the animals to Adams so that he could name them. God said to Adam, what ever you call it, that will be their name. What situation are you facing today? What mountain are you facing that seem impossible to climb? I dare you to speak to it. What ever you call it, that's what it will be. Our biggest mistake is going to God telling him about how big our problem is, rather than to tell the enemy how big our God is. That is why the mountain is not moving because the angel will only do exploits to the things that you give voice to according to the Word because Heaven is voice activated by the Word!

❧❦❧

Don't just listen to God's word. You must do what it says. Otherwise, you are only fooling yourselves. For if you listen to the word and don't obey, it is like glancing at your face in the mirror. You see yourself, walk away, and forget what you look like. But the perfect law sets you free, and if you do what it says and don't forget what you heard, then God will bless you for doing it. (James 1:22-25 NLT)

❧❦❧

His word is perfect, meaning it is complete, pure, flawless and it has transforming power to transform your image supernaturally into the spiritual image that you are beholding. Remember the cliché "whatever you behold, you become". His word is powerful to change you and it sets you free. If you are anything like I was, this was all new to me. I kept saying to myself "set me free from what? I am not bound. Like most people, I thought I was getting alone pretty good. I now tell people that I didn't know that I needed to be saved until he saved me. I sat in church for many years and did not know what it really meant to be saved. I had not heard the whole gospel story. You may be like I was, so I will take my time and share some tools and show you how to get your dominion back. You will have to fight for it because the enemy will not just release it back into your hands. Why? because you gave him legal access into your life

Who do they say that you are?

We talked earlier about what people are saying about Jesus, but what are people saying about you? Would they say that you are you a disciple which means student, follower, or disciplined learner? The world will quickly tell you who you are not! if you claim to be a Christian but are not following the commandments of God. The world will pick up on that very quickly if you are not authentic. Why is that? Because that is how the world is without Christ, therefore they can identify with that characteristic because it is very familiar to them. It is a given fact the world is always watching even when you think that they are not. Just like the Pharisee always waiting to catch Jesus in a trap. The world is looking for authenticity, people who are real. People with unmasked faces, I'd like to call it. If Christ is in you and you are in Christ, your life should be changing because of the connection. Salvation should not be a stopping point, but the beginning of greater works. The process between salvation and greater works is called change. Salvation is the foundation which is the beginning of something great, but change is the process that God uses to empower you to do greater things. It is utterly impossible to truly receive salvation and not change. Think about it, what does it mean to you to be "saved". Everybody has their own interpretation of what salvation mean, or what it does not mean. When I read the scriptures, it lets me know that we are moving further and further away from the true intent of the Word of God. Salvation does not only mean that you get to go to heaven. That would be great if that was all that it meant. Yes, going to heaven is a benefit, but if that was all there was to it; God would have saved you and taken you to heaven the very day you received salvation. He left you here for a reason.

***

"I tell you the truth, anyone who believes in me will do the same works I have done, and even greater works, because I am going to be with the Father. You can ask for anything in my name, and I will do it, so that the Son can bring glory to the Father". (John 14:12-13 NLT)

***

He wants you to do "Greater works" on the earth, but you cannot do greater works if you are bound. Something supernaturally happens when you receive salvation. It is so supernatural that you may not ever be able to explain it, but you will know when you receive it because there is a supernatural change that occur on impact. You may not feel anything, but the transformation process has begun because God works outside of the natural realm of things which are your five senses (sight, smell taste, touch, hear). The Greek word for transformation is *metamorphoo* which is to change from one state of being to another, like the caterpillar changing into a beautiful butterfly. Did you know that all butterflies are not the same, but have different colors and their colors are associated with how long they stay in the cocoon? See, God has it all figured out. Basically, like you and I, no two butterflies are the same. There is not a set time for the butterfly to emerge from the cocoon. One thing I do know for certain is this – Once the butterfly emerges, it can never go back to being a caterpillar. That is the awesomeness of God. Letting go of your past may be painfully hard, not just for you but for all of us. You've got to know that God is trying to get you to a place that He has already carved out for you. It is imperative that you agree with him and embrace change so that you do not abort the process. The butterfly does not decide when he is coming out, it is only when the process has been complete that the butterfly will emerge.

The car industry is always looking for ways to improve and change the model of their cars at least every three years to make them more affordable and reliable. Most fashion designers change their styles due to the ever- growing trends, much like the business industry who changes their strategies at least every three to five years to improve the quantity and the quality of their business and stay one step ahead of the game. Change comes by faith and you must know that you don't have to do it alone because there is Grace available to help you through the process. Most people want a quick fix but they are not willing to go through the process. You've made every attempt to change yourself not knowing that the outward change is only temporary. Yes, you may look better and even feel great, but give it some time, you will revert right back to your old self. If your roof is leaking, at some point you are going to have to stop patching it and get a new roof. To keep patching the roof when you know that you have the money to get it fixed tells me that you are either lazy or cheap. That's how most people treat their salvation, like it is nothing important so they never aspire to do anything else. They think in their minds that magically everything will just fall into place, and all they must do is just exist and God will do the rest. I am sorry to say, but it doesn't work like that. God has already done his part when he sent his son from heaven to earth. My question to you is "What have you done since you confessed your hope in Christ." You should not be in the same place today where you were a year or two ago, naturally or spiritually. This will be a good place for you to pause and look back over at least the last five years of your life and see if your life has changed for the better. Time and chance will always intersect giving you an opportunity to change directions or positions, but because we do not recognize change we allow it to slip away because it is unfamiliar. Please are so comfortable where they are that they are afraid to do anything different.

There are typically two types of people:

o People who acknowledge they need to change but may not know how to.

o People who acknowledge they need to change but refuse to.

Change is not considered change until you change positions and actively do something different other than what you have been doing. Jesus came not only to change your life, but to exchange your old life for a new one. To give you a new life that you have never had before by extending to man the plan of salvation. Your season of pretense is over and you can no longer claim to be something that you are not unless you change. It is amazing to know that the God of the universe, creator of all things, the eternal God by His grace has given us a blueprint to change. Salvation has afforded us an invitation not only to receive salvation and live in eternity with him forever, but to impact the kingdom of darkness with the kingdom of light while on earth. Christian standards will provoke radical change in you because it is only by following the Biblical principles that change comes. In the Old Testament whenever someone would sin, they must bring God a sacrifice to appease him. The life of an animal had to be sacrificed to cover the sin of the people. In the Levitical law, an animal had to lose his life for payment of the wrongs you committed. How many animals lost their life just this week alone for the things you did wrong if animal sacrifice was will necessary. How many half-truths did you tell this week. Some people call off sick from their jobs just to sleep in late How many times have you lied, claim to be sick, cheating, stealing and so on? Think about that for a moment because sin has consequences and separates us from the presence of God, in the Old Testament when that happened they had to kill an animal. Most people only know the ten commandments, but there were over 600 laws in the Old Testament that could not be violated. Sin is not only doing what is wrong, but it is also not doing what you know to do that is right. Now through the atoning work of his son on the cross, repentance brings us back into fellowship. Ultimately it was sin that drove Adam and Eve out of the Garden, not the fruit. Yes - the fruit played apart, but it was their pride, rebellion and disobedience.

And she will have a son and you are to name him Jesus, for he will save *the people from their sins.* (Mat 1:21 NLT)

Jesus was the sacrifice that paid for the sins of whole world. He was the lamb that was slain before the foundation of the world. The bible says that we have all sinned and come short of the Glory of God. Most of the new generation charismatic churches are teaching that sin is simply "missing the mark" but it is more than about missing the mark? I remember hearing a message once like that and I remember wondering, what is that all about. So many times, we want to try and lessen the effects of reality to take the sting away. No one wants to talk about sin because it puts the accountability back where it belongs, back on you. Jesus did not suffer a cruel and inhumane death at the hands of Pontus Pilate who served as the Roman Governor of Judea because I missed the mark. To me, it is more precious than that. He died to save me from my sin. The ultimate effects of his death were to bring change and provide a solution for a dying world. In the Hebrew context, sin is hata, pesha or aveira which means to trespass or sin out of rebellion or transgression or sin done out of moral failing. It was later transcribed by the Greek to mean missing the mark in the New Testament.

When we live beneath what Christ has died for, it's like telling him "what you have done was not enough." If that is your case, you are saying that the Bible is not true, therefore it takes away your accountability to do what the word say: Be Holy.

CHAPTER TWO
Living Out Your Confession

Living the Celebrated Life

There is always a reason to celebrate. The angels in heaven celebrate over one sinner who gives their life to Christ. We celebrate anniversaries, birthdays, holidays, births, graduations and even death. Most traditional funerals are being done away with and they are being called "The celebration of life" to honor the life and memory of the deceased person. Now days people are just coming up with things to celebrate like: Ground Hog Day, Grandparents Day, Cancer Awareness Day. I have fond memories growing up and being invited to a birthday party. We were taught to take a gift to honor the guest of honor. I don't really see much of that anymore, but even to this day I always show up with a gift to honor the honoree. Receiving an invitation was something that came with great anticipation and was not taken lightly, but with joy and gratitude. There is a tremendous amount of details that goes into planning, such as time, money and effort just to prepare a celebration and making a guest list. Society has somehow done away with bringing a gift to a celebration, but everyone wants to have to good time at someone else's expense. Salvation is your invitation to know God, the father. You are invited into a personal relationship with him and a chance to live in the kingdom.

Have you ever received a gift from someone maybe around the holidays, but never open it up to see what is in the box? Do you still gifts still wrapped and stored in the closet, on the shelf or in the attic? I use to work with a lady that would take her unwanted gifts, rewrap them and give them away to someone for the next Christmas. How unappreciative and distasteful is that. When was the last time you bought someone a gift or maybe someone bought you one? There is a lot that goes into picking out the perfect gift based on the purpose and the intent of the giver. When was the last time you stood in a long line at the department store, or shopped on line hoping that the gift will be delivered in time? There was a time that I would not buy anything online because I have always like to see what I am buying. Shopping online was confusing and time consuming. Now my sister on the other she will buy everything on line. She will pull up multiple screens and find the competitor website and coupons.

Salvation is the perfect gift given by God to the world. This was the most expensive and extravagant gift that could be given when He sent his son Jesus into the world that we may have life. It is the gift of love and no one is excluded from receiving the invitation, everyone is invited to the celebration of Life. You are free to live life to its fullest and experience all that God has for you. There is an extraordinary life awaiting those who put their trust in Jesus. I admonish you to be a participator and not a spectator because Salvation come by faith in Jesus Christ. The confession of your faith is in your mouth.

"That if you confess with your mouth the Lord Jesus and believe in your heart that God has raised him from the dead, you will be saved" For with the heart, one believes unto righteousness, and with the mouth confession is made unto salvation. For the scriptures says, "Whosoever believes on Him will not be put to shame". (Roman 10:9-11 NIV)

You must live out your confession, your confession must be actively working in your life. If you witness and testify that you are saved, you should live like it. There should be an outward manifestation of your confession. Many of the people in Jesus day and even today only want to claim him as savior because he rescued them continuously from the enemy. When you are faced with a situation or a crisis in your life where you feel helpless or defeated. Who do you call on to deliver you? God is a mighty deliverer and whosoever shall call upon his name shall be saved. If God does not intervene on your behalf, you will not make it. Desperate times calls for desperate measures and in your hour of despair you call on the Lord to save or deliver you which He does by His grace because of His faithfulness. Maybe you went the loss of a job or the loss of a love one or some other type of tragedy to happen in your life and God brought you out by his strength. You know him to be a savior. He wants salvation to not be a stopping point or a resting place, but the beginning of something great". Jesus said "greater works shall you do because I go to my father". Salvation is the beginning of something new that you have never ever experienced before. Salvation is just the beginning of the kingdom life which comes with an unlimited amount of resources to help you along this journey. You were predestined for salvation, and you probably hear the term a lot "predestination". Salvation was not an afterthought or plan B, but it was always the intent of the father that we would live forever as eternal beings in his presence. It was already pre-determined that we would be saved and Jesus would be sacrificed to save us. God is known by so many names and maybe you know him only as savior if he has saved you. Some call his name Jehovah Jireh if he has provided a way out of no way. Maybe last year you knew him as Jehovah Rapha, your healer. Perhaps he is your sanctifier. My point is there may be one name that stands out more than another based on how God has dealt with you. Maybe you have never experienced him in any other way. He wants to be more than just savior, and my prayer is that you know him in a more intimate way.

Either he is Lord of All or not Lord at All. God want to be Lord over your life and not just Savior, but you must allow Him access. Lord means ruler, supreme authority which is where the word landlord or land owner is originated from. A landlord is one who owns the property and not just the house or dwelling place, but they also own the land that the house is sitting on. Before a tenet move in they normally sign a lease agreement agreeing to pay a certain amount each month, normally for one year. This is binding contract that have been mutually agreed upon and signed by both parties pointing out the rights and responsibilities of the tenet and owner that they both must abide by. The landlord or land owner have certain rights to the property and in most states can enter the property at any time. The owner of the property can assign the tenet where to park and can even evict you if you have any unauthorized people living with you whose name is not on the lease. It is the responsibility of the Landlord to make sure the dwelling place is kept clean and inhabitable condition. Smoke detectors must be installed on every level for the safety of the tenets, and the paint would be tested for lead which is very harmful and can cause defects in children, in most states. Our Lord is a greater example of a natural landlord because when we make him the Lord of our lives, he provides safety, security and provision. When you receive salvation, you receive the Holy Spirit that comes to live in your heart and he is like a smoke detector. The fire detector warns you before the fire, at the first smell of smoke. The Holy Spirit will do the same thing regarding people, places, and things that tries to intervene in your life without his permission. When the enemy come in like a flood, the Spirit of the Lord will raise a standard against him.

The righteousness of God has been revealed through love and it has nothing to do with your education, culture, social status, association or affiliation. Society tends to exclude certain people by making them feel inferior or invaluable based on the type of car you drive, how much money you have, type of cloths you wear, or the geographical area you live in. This leprosy has infiltrated our churches causing clicks even in the church which cause spiritual bondage. It can cause you to feel like you do not fit in "the church", or you are not good enough to function in certain roles by the church standards which is known as church hurt. I have been to places like that I walked away more damaged, than when I first came in. Don't ever let that discourage you because God is showing you that you are not supposed to fit in. You will never fit into any mold that society has determined acceptable for you. I dare to be different. Every year there are marriage counselling and seminars on how to keep your marriage together everywhere you look. Where are the seminars and conference inviting people that are struggling with fear or addictions? Who is teaching and embracing those with real issues and problems and helping them work through them. When I first got saved, this was all new to me and that is how I recognize that we are out of balance. Have you looked lately where it seemed there is a revival and the only ones that show up are the church folk that should already be on fire. Where does the unchurched fit in? We need balance, sometimes we tend to focus on one area and not enough on another area. If we focus more on Lord Jesus, he will give us wisdom and show us what to do. There are certain standards and values that have crept into the church unaware that has shaped our thinking and action to reflect the ways of this world, and we have made this the standard of righteousness. God initially called the Jewish people to be his chosen people. God's choosing of that nationality and race had nothing to do with them, but everything to do with God. God could have chosen any nation, but He chose them, therefore they could not boast about themselves. Apart from God, within yourself there is nothing that you can offer God. He never looked over the face of the earth and saw that they were more acceptable or they were more separated or anything that you could imagine. They were like everyone else on the planet, but out of the kindness, goodness, love and compassion of his heart he chose them. Never Let the position that you hold define who you are because it quickly become pride but realize that you are only where you are in life is all because of God. Some churches count all the people that come to service every Sunday and use the number of people that attended service as an indicator that the church is growing. It doesn't matter how large the church membership is if all the members are unconverted. A healthy church is known by the number of conversions, not the number of people on the role.

❧

The Lord did not set His affection on you or choose you because you were more numerous than any other people, for you were the fewest of all peoples. But it was because the Lord loved you and kept the oath he swore to your forefathers that he brought you out with a mighty hand and redeemed you from the land of slavery. From the power of Pharaoh king of Egypt. Know, therefore that the Lord your God is God. He is the faithful God, keeping his covenant of love to a thousand generations of those who love him and keep his commandment. (Due 7:7-9 NIV)

❧

Salvation is defined as "saving of a person from sin or its consequences especially in the life after death". The saving from danger, difficulty or evil; something that saves. Since the death of Jesus, salvation is not only just for the Jews, but also for the gentiles. While we were yet sinners Jesus died for us; making salvation not attainable by works, because it is a gift and you only need to receive it by faith.

❧

You see, at just the right time when we were still powerless, Christ died for ungodly. Very rarely will anyone die for a righteous man, though for a good man someone might possible dare to die. But God demonstrates his own love for us in this: While we were still sinners Christ died for us. Since we have now been justified by his blood, how much more shall we be saved from God's wrath through him! For if, when we were Gods enemies, we were reconciled to him through the death of his Son. How much more, having been reconciled, shall we be saved through his life!(Romans 5:6-10 NIV)

❧

Apostle Paul made it very clear that he is sent by God and not himself to preach the good news of Jesus Christ. In those days, Apostles had to be "sent by God" but there were some that were ordained "by men". Paul wanted to make sure that you know that there is a difference and we have somehow gotten confused. Just because you call yourself a pastor and start a church, does not mean that you are a pastor if you have not received the call by God. Remember in the book of Acts it shows how the twelve disciples went on to become Apostles and advanced the kingdom. Paul was excited to hear about their faith and how it was spreading throughout the world. They had put their faith into action, they are doing the things that they were taught and God was increasing them. Multiplication and increase comes only when you are actively doing something. They were able to take the knowledge which is information they learned and applied it to their lives, that's wisdom. In Paul's prayer he always made mention of them because of their faith and he was passionate for an opportunity just to be able to go and visit so they could share their faith and build each other up personally. Paul was eager to share the gospel, teach and impart spiritual gifts to them that will help them stand firm in the faith. We should all be able to identify with Paul not because he was an apostle, but we all go through test and trials and tribulations in our lives and need to be encouraged and lifted. God created humanity for an earthly relationship which is symbolic of the heavenly relationship in the trinity, there is unity in the Spirit. You may not have figured it out yet but you are a relational being and not an island off to yourself. Paul heard about their faith, but he need to see them, there are some things that people cannot share over the phone. Have you ever had a sick child or parent or maybe spouse in the hospital and things are not looking good. Normally the physician will not tell you about their condition over the phone. "They will tell you, you need to get to the hospital right away!" The disciples did not travel alone for that very reason, they were sent out by two's. If one is down, the other can lift them up. In this life there is going to come a time that you are going to need someone to lift you up and encourage you. You may not think so right now because you are in a good place. It would be utterly impossible to go through life and this not happen because God designed it this way. Paul needed some encouragement, he had been shipwrecked, beaten and left for dead, thrown out of the city and put in prison all for preaching the gospel. Apostle Paul constantly stressed that salvation came because of the love the father has for mankind and it has nothing to do with our love for the father. It was grace that saved us. We were God's enemies, there was nothing good in us, everything about our nature was vile and corrupt. Our deeds were evil, our thoughts were evil and our imaginations were vain. Everything that we devised came from a wicked heart, impure motives and intent. Even in the depraved state of being, the father looked down and because of His mercy and grace He never changed His mind about us. You know how most people do, if they have good thoughts about you they would make you a cake, buy you something nice, take you out to eat or send you a card in the mail. If they were upset at you because of what you did, what you forgot to do or what you said ……. You would also know. Their attitude toward you would change, you may see the reaction on their face, hear it in their voice or see it in their body language. Your actions are a depiction of your thoughts and they are not easily hidden although some people try to master it. Think about how many people you were nice to because they were nice to you. Now think about how many people you were mean to, just because they were mean to you. Thank God that he is not like that. Even when we were unlovable, he still loved us enough to save us. His first thoughts that he has ever had about you was good and it will always be good. His thoughts are that you will reign and rule on the earth, have dominion, conquer and subdue. In other words, bring heaven to earth. The scriptures said we were justified, which means God has declared you righteous when you receive His son by faith and because of that you can stand in confidence. To save someone, you must be stronger than the one that you are saving otherwise it won't work. I remember when my son was a little boy and I was doing something around the house and I tripped. He had to be about five years old. he reached out his little hand and said" I'll save you mommy". That was so cute, but I knew that he could not save me because he was not strong enough. We were without strength and in need of a savior and it had to be someone that was stronger and more powerful than ourselves. According to God's standard, when Christ died for the sins of the world, our sin was beyond reproach. They had stacked up so high that they had reached the heavens. Take a moment and think about every person that crossed your path. Are there any that you would be willing to give your life for?

Consider a righteous man or a man in right standing and following the ways of the Lord. Just to paint a better picture, a righteous man would be like a person who is in church every Sunday, teaching Sunday school, helping in Children's ministry and occasionally driving the church van for the outreach program. If this righteous man was given a death sentence and you could volunteer to take his place so that you could die in his place, would you volunteer? Better yet, how many volunteers would be eager to come forth. There are a lot of people on death row, and some have died or been executed that were righteous. Paul said scarcely for a righteous man will one die.

For a good man, the chances of someone volunteering to die in your place is even slimmer. A good man today would be considered a man or woman of good moral character. A good man is not necessarily a follower of Jesus Christ but can be an upstanding citizen in the community. This person is a hard worker, very respectful, have no allegations pending on their name. They have not been slandered and are well respected by their peers. It does not matter how good or religious you are, people are not just willing to forsake their families to die for you. Jesus died for the ungodly, that is amazing. I don't know of anybody who would do that. The "ungodly" is any person separated from God, any person that does not acknowledge Him as God, or creator. Any Person who does not follow Him or seek the will of the father for their life. I know that you have heard the term ungodly and some people use it rather loosely. It is a person who is totally in opposition to God's standards, laws, commandments and precepts. I challenge you to go throughout the neighborhood and knock on every door. Take a poll or survey to see how many people would be willing to die in exchange for a murderer, a person that is rebellious, selfish, or a thief. You will most likely get no volunteers.

The point Paul is driving home is, No one is eager to risk their life and leave their family behind to die for a person that is religious or good. The chances of getting a volunteer to die for a man that has committed a crime is unheard of. The good news is that there is a God that is so loving that he includes everyone and no one is excluded from the plan of salvation. It does not matter what you have done, where you have been, or where you have come from. God sent His son Jesus to die in your place. What an awesome God that we serve that looked down on humanity and being moved with compassion came down to save us. Because of his great love for us we are to reciprocate the love back to him. God loves to tabernacle with man so that we can live in peace and harmony on the earth, to subdue, multiply and have dominion over all the living creatures on the earth. In the book of Genesis, it tells us that when God created man, he was created outside of the garden, but God placed man inside the garden which is a metaphor of God's presence and salvation brings us back into the presence of God because of the righteousness of Jesus Christ that we receive through faith. When God looks at you he sees his son, therefore to commune with God it is a necessity that you have His Spirit. God is a Spirit and they that worship him must worship him in Spirit and in Truth. We are living in the dispensation that the Spirit of God has been poured out

⋆⋆⋆

And afterward, I will pour my Spirit on all people. Your sons and daughters will prophesy, your old men will dream dreams, your young men will see visions. Even on my servants, both men and women I will pour out my Spirit in those day. (Joel 2:28-29 NIV)

⋆⋆⋆

God created everything to thrive in the sphere for which He created it for. The marine kingdom was created to thrive in water. The birds were created to fly and thrive high up in the sky, looking over valleys and mountains. The animal kingdom was created to thrive off the land, but man was created to thrive only in the presence of the Lord. A fish taken out of water will eventually die because water to a fish is his oxygen, his life source. I must share this encounter with you and hopefully you will get the revelation of what God is speaking to you, right now. I pulled in at a gas station about three years ago, and when I got out of my car and proceeded to pump my gas, I looked down and there in front of the pump was a gold fish lying on the ground. I suspected he was dead because he was not moving. I could tell that he had not been there very long because his color was still very vibrant. I kept thinking to myself, "the gas stating is a strange place to find a gold fish on the ground". My immediate thought was, perhaps some child getting out of the car with their parent dropped it. I proceeded to ask the Holy Spirit about this fish.

I am so analytical, I wanted to know how he got there and how did he die. This is what the Holy Spirt revealed. He said, "The fish is out of its element, a fish cannot survive outside the environment it was created for." This goes back to the Book of Genesis where God gave the fish, "water" as its habitation to thrive in. Remember when I pointed out that God "placed man in the garden". That is your habitation. Its his presence! You will only be able to thrive in his presence. The water to a fish is his oxygen which is the life support or supply. It does not matter how the fish got there. What ever place you are in life, you will die spiritually if you are outside your element. You will be able to tell relatively quickly because things will begin to dry up (relationships, business, finance,) You will struggle in a place that you are not called into. It is in his presence that I am made whole.

You must be born again

I am glad that you asked that question. You must be born again! Earlier I mentioned that there is a process between Salvation and doing the Greater Works and it is called change. Well, this is how you change. Going to church can't change you, your pastor can not change you and momma can't change you. Even reading the bible, can't change you. Those are great tools used as an invitation to change, but they won't change you. The change that I am talking about is from the inside out. It is drastic, and it is radical. It is like a head-on collision. You cannot be in a head-on collision and your body not be affected by change in one way or another. Have you ever heard someone tell you about someone who has been in a car accident? When you ask how they are doing, their reply is "they walked away without a scratch". That would mean that the effects of the car accident left no "visible signs." Signs such as scrapes, scratches, bumps or bruises that could be seen with the natural eye. In all actuality, something did just happen it just have not manifested yet because it is internal. That would be how the new birth experience is. It is slow and gradual, after receiving salvation.

CREST

There was a man of the Pharisees named Nicodemus, a ruler of the Jewish ruling council. He came to Jesus at night and said, Rabbi, we know you are a teacher who has come from God. For no one could perform the miraculous signs you are doing if God were not with him." In reply Jesus declared, "I tell you the truth, unless a man is born again, he cannot see the kingdom of God. "How can a man be born when he is old?" Nicodemus asked. "Surely he cannot enter a second time into his mother's womb to be born!" Jesus answered, "I tell you the truth, unless a man is born of water and the Spirit, he cannot enter the kingdom of God. Flesh gives birth to flesh, but the Spirit gives birth to spirit. You should not be surprised at my saying, you must be born again. The wind blows wherever it pleases. You hear its sound, but you cannot tell where it comes from or where it is going. So, it is with everyone born of the Spirit." "How can this be?" Nicodemus asked. "You are Israel's teacher," said Jesus, "and do you not understand these things? I tell you the truth, we speak of what we know, and we testify to what we have seen, but still you people do not accept our testimony. (John 3: 1-11NIV)

Nicodemus was a Pharisee and a member of the Sanhedrin. The Pharisees were a group from the Jewish sect, teachers of the law that believed in the resurrection. The New Testament in the synoptic gospels it talks a lot about the Pharisee how they religiously went about fasting, gave tithes and offering, prayed loud religiously and went to all the festivals just for the sake of keeping the law. You can make the Word of God a ritual and never experience the redemptive work of Holy Spirit to conform you into the image of Christ. When Jesus spoke to the disciples on the sermon on the mount, he wanted to make sure that they understood that their righteousness must far surpass the righteousness of the Pharisee to enter the kingdom of God. Paul goes on to say in one of his letters to the church in Philippi that he was a Pharisee because Paul wanted them to know how religious he was before he had an encounter with Jesus. It is a fact, you cannot have an encounter with Jesus and stay the same. It is impossible! The Pharisees knew the word and could quote it, but they could not live by it. They held the law of Moses far above their belief in God whom Moses wrote about. This caused their attitudes to become external, religious and mechanical. They had an outward form of worship and thought by keeping the law that they were saved, isn't that like most people in the church today who have the same misconception. There are some people who go to church Sunday after Sunday, but they are not living the life they just sang about in the choir fifteen minutes ago. We go through all these religious acts for nothing and are only fooling ourselves. The Worship Leader tells you to lift your hands and sing unto the Lord, "I surrender All". You sing the song like you have, but you know that you really have not "surrender all", but you are singing like you have. Right there with your hands lifted would be a good place to be honest and tell God "I have not surrender all, but today I give it all to you". There are still some things that you are holding on to that you do not want to surrender. Just be honest with God and let him know that you really would like to surrender all, but it's hard. He already knows! Even church can become an idol if you are going for the wrong reason. You probably did not know that you could go to church "for the wrong reason". When I use the word wrong reason, it is to say "what are the intents of the heart". "What is the real reason for going to church". Here are just a few examples that will help to better explain it. Are you going to church?

- To be seen by others just for the sake of going.

- To be a part of a group and connect with people

- To feel accepted by people

If your motive for going to church is not to meet with the true a living God and to be transformed (to be changed), you are going for the wrong reason. Church cannot change an individual, only God can. I must keep saying this over and over. Only God can change you. I can testify to that because It took me a good while to finally realize that I too was a picture of the Pharisees. I was doing all the right things, but for the wrong reason. If you are going to church out of habit, tradition or any customary pattern such as, you went to church as a child and now you are still going. You are religious.! t is a known fact that everyone in church is not converted, although it took me a long time to see that. I was just so excited to be saved and apart of this new family. Once I started reading the bible I could not believe what was in there. Some of the things that I read, I had to quickly shut the bible, catch my breath after waiting a couple of minutes before opening it up again. I said to myself, the Lord has a lot of work to do on me because I need a complete overhaul. Do you know anyone like that, who is faithful to the traditions of man rather than their commitment to God?

CRAFT\#SDO

"Making the word of God to no effect through our traditions which you have handed down, and much such things you do. (Mark 7:13 NKJV)

CRAFT\#SDO

Nicodemus was of man of good moral character, like most people today if you were to ask them. Being a good person does not ensure you a ticket to heaven, you must be born again. You can go to church all year and not miss one service, serve in the community where you live, feed the hungry and clothe the poor, visit the sick and sign up for a mission trip. All those things make you feel pretty good about yourself and what you have done, but good works cannot save you! The teaching of Jesus and his disciples were in total opposition of what the Pharisees was teaching. He was try to transition them from religion to relationship and trying to get them to a place that they would have a desire to know the God that they served. How can you trust a God that you do not know? Salvation is solely because of the grace of God, through your faith and not your good works.

Rebirth or Born again is a term that is most often used and it is not an easy subject to talk about or understand. For the most part, we may never fully understand everything about it because rebirth is supernatural. Being born again is a command or requirement, it is necessary to experience eternal life. Jesus was not making a suggestion, therefore being regenerated is not an option for a believer. Nicodemus was struggling with this profound truth that Jesus was revealing about rebirth which sounds strange. "What exactly are you saying", Nicodemus must have thought to himself. I have never heard of such a thing. I was the same way years ago when I first started reading about this new birth experience, and you probably were to. We are all that way when we hear something that just bypasses the natural understanding of all five senses. Nicodemus affirmed with certainty that Jesus came from God because of the signs and miracles that he was performing, only God can do those things. His conclusion of the matter was correct. Jesus said, you *"must be"* born again to see the kingdom of God. There is no other alternative, if you want to experience and be a partaker of the heavenly kingdom of God and experience eternal life, be victorious and an overcomer you must be born again. It is not negotiable or debatable. This kingdom is a personal experience and it is not just for the Jews. This is not an earthly kingdom like they supposed, but this kingdom will be in you.

We have not fully grasped the concept, nor have we made it a living reality that Kingdom is a two-part word which means "king – dominion". It means to live as a citizen of a community that is governed by a king. We hear the word "church" so much that we think the church is the kingdom, but it is not. You can be in the church, but not in the kingdom. The king's dominion will be in your heart and it will transform you from the inside out regardless of race, color or creed. The rebirth experience transfers Kingdom Dominion back into the hands of every believer which was God's original plan for man.

And he asked them, "Did you receive the Holy Spirit when you believed?" they answered, "No, we have not even heard that there is a Holy Spirit. (Acts 19:2 NIV)

God of the Universe wants you to bring the culture of the kingdom from Heaven and establish it on the earth.

Nicodemus could not understand outside of his five sense and I can imagine the look on Nicodemus face when Jesus made the statement because Jesus said to him "do not be amazed or astonished when I say, you must be born again". Every person on earth was born naturally through the womb of a woman which is by water which is the first birth. Some Theologians might suppose that the first birth by water could mean baptism when a new believer is immersed in water after the repentance of sin. I am not here to debate either one. In other words, the first birth is what happens to a natural man. The second birth that Jesus is talking about is spiritual and happens supernaturally. This rebirth will take place by the Holy Spirit and there are many symbolisms used to describe the Person of the Holy Spirit such as wind or breath. Have you ever watched the weather forecast and the news meteorologist predicted a storm has been spotted on the radar and it is moving at alarming speed? The meteorologist may even give the details about what direction it's coming from and how long it will last. Suddenly, the meteorologist comes back with another weather advisory alerting you the storm took an unusual turn and headed in an opposite direction and advise you to take cover! That would be a good analogy of the Spirit that Jesus is telling Nicodemus about. The meteorologist can predict the wind based on all the education and all the high technological equipment we now have access to. The Spirit, being the Holy Spirit is not controlled by man because it is the Spirit of God. Can you imagine what would happen if man could control or manipulate God? You would put yourself on the throne and everyone else would be beneath you. There would be so much wickedness and injustice. How do I know, because the heart of man is prideful and deceitfully wicked? That is why you must be born again. New birth is invisible, you cannot see the wind, but you will be able to see the lasting effects of the wind left by the damage. If you are not born again like the bible say, you are natural and can only understand natural things. Spiritual things can only be discerned spiritually.

❧❧❧

The man without the Spirit does not accept the things that come from the Spirit of God, for they are foolishness to him, and he cannot understand them, because they are spiritually discerned. The spiritual man makes judgements about all things, but he himself is not subject to any man's judgement. (1 Cor 2:14-15 NIV)

❧❧❧

When you repent with your whole heart and believe in Jesus you received the new birth experience and with this new experience comes spiritual benefits.

o The power to become Holy

o A new path and destiny

o You have been translated from the kingdom of darkness into the kingdom of light

o You have been forgiven of your sin

Most people would argue that once you receive salvation that everything is wiped away! You have a new start. You are brand new. I heard that so many times but did not understand at first how it fit together. When Jesus died, I was forgiven for anything that I have done up to that point that I received him as my savior. Although his atoning work cover my past, present and future mistakes I was only concerned about my past. I had not given the present or future mistakes much thought because I had not gotten that far yet. I knew my life had not been a good life up to that point, so I just wanted to start there.

⟮◦⟯

What shall we say, then? Shall we go on sinning so that grace may increase? By no means! We died in sin; how can we live in it any longer. (Romans 6:1 NIV)

⟮◦⟯

You are not going to have a desire to continue in sin if you are truly saved. The Holy Spirit begins to wash that desire away and he conforms you into the image of Christ.

Forgiveness is always made available no matter what stage on this journey you are at if you repent from a pure heart. The results or the trauma that was caused by my act of sin, which I like to call "consequences" are still there. If you are incarcerated for committing a murder, you may never get out. Does that mean that you are not forgiven.? No, you could have committed the most detestable crime and pray to God in all sincerity of heart and repent. He will hear your cry and forgive your sins. Just because you are forgiven of sins, does not mean you "get out of jail free". Now in the same sense, God is so powerful that he can issue a pardon on your behalf if he chooses to. I say this so strong because a lot of things I heard over the years, I am finding today were so misleading. Let me use another example: If you smoked cigarettes and drank alcohol and was diagnosed with lung or liver cancer. Does God forgive you when you get saved? Yes, he forgives you for the abuse that you have done to your body, but that does not mean that cancer will be gone immediately. God can heal you from cancer instantly, but the point I am making is the cancer may be the consequences that resulted from your choice to smoke or consume alcohol. I will use this last example to shed a little light from a different angle. If you are married and commit an adulterous act and contract a communicable disease, does God forgive you? if you pray from sincerity of heart and repent, he will forgive your sin but you may live the rest of your life with the disease because of the choices you made. Deliverance is a separate experience from salvation and is a vital part of our spirituality.

Deliverance and salvation goes hand in hand and work together to bring you total freedom and liberty so that you can actively walk it out. Receiving the Holy Spirit and being baptized in the Holy Spirit also goes hand in hand, but they are two different experiences and you will need them both. To function in the full capacity that God has called you to walk in, you will need to be baptized in the Holy Ghost. When I first became a Christian, all I knew was that I was saved, and I never knew that there was so much more to salvation than what I was experiencing. I could not tell you how it happened or what happened. I had been in and out of church since I was a young child, but it was not until I became an adult that I pursued a personal relationship with the Lord. My mom would get us ready and take us to church every Sunday. It wasn't long before church became our second home and a refuge for us. I sang in the choir about a God that I did not know.

I remember in my mind even as a child when I thought about heaven, I would imagine the streets paved with gold, angels singing, I could see the twelve gates to the city, this radiant glow of light and this place was high in the sky. I heard the songs about "you will never get tired or grow old", "no more sickness there" and how God is going to wipe away every tear from your eye. Heaven was a place to be desired. People talked about it, they sang about it and they taught and wrote about it. I was confident that there was a heaven and that I was going there one day, but I could not quite understand what I needed to do to get there.

You don't hear many sermons about heaven anymore. When was the last time you heard a sermon about heaven? It is almost as if we have become so consumed with this life on earth that heaven is just a memory we once had. We are doing other things and can't quite seem to fit God into the schedule. We have replaced the glory of God for idol worship. Anything that you take pride in due to self-efforts are idols. You cannot replace the revelation of God with intellectual information by earning degrees, and platforms. You cannot grow the church by coming up with witty ideas to increase your membership role. I've seen some churches turn the lights down low a blow fog during Praise and Worship to create the effects like you are at a live concert. They got valet parking and reserved seating. Some atmospheres are so casuals, people are eating and drinking in the sanctuary. Commercialism is sweeping the nation and the churches are being marketed out as a business.

Except the Lord build the house, he who labors, labors in vain. It may last for a while, but it will soon come to not. Go back to the basic of trusting God for all thin

CHAPTER THREE
It Belongs to Me

Deliverance is the children's bread

Everything you get in this life, you will have to fight for it. You will also have to fight to keep it. You fight every day for the simplest things that you may not even be aware of. You literally fight for peace and joy every day because there is always something that happens whether at home or on the job that will shift your attitude. When faced with a chaotic situation, it will be struggle for you to remain peaceful when your first inclination is to go off. You must make a conscious decision to take control of the situations around you. When I was in the Army, our motto was blood, sweat and tears. That motto speaks volumes to me today because during the struggles of life, it may cost you - your life (blood), energy (sweat) and sorrows (tears). There is an invisible world and an invisible war and you are automatically engaged in without any knowledge or warning. Salvation leads to spiritual warfare just in case you have not noticed. Things were not that chaotic before you got saved. At times they were, but you just figured "that's life", so it was more acceptable. You cannot see your opponent with the natural eye, and it bypasses the understanding of your natural mind, but his works are manifested naturally through people and circumstances. To engage the enemy or any opponent you must acknowledge there is an enemy and know the rules on how to engage him.

You are a spirit being and your spirit contacts spiritual things. You have a soul which is your mind, will and emotions which are the parts of man used for reasoning to contact mental or natural things. You have five senses which are hearing, sight, smell, taste and touch which allows you to contact physical things. Your five senses teach your brain to respond because your brain depend on your five senses and cannot function without them. When you are born again, your spirit is recreated and your spirit has authority over your soul and body. It may not seem like it at first, but it does. Through the power of the Holy Spirit your soul and body will have to be taught that it has lost its dominion. The bible speaks a lot about the old man and the new man or the old heart and the new heart in the old and new testament. The dominion of the old man is lost by deliverance! Deliverance belongs to every believer, it's in the contract. There are some things that you can voluntarily give up like drug, sex, pornography, gambling or whatever habit you had prior to being saved. Just because you gave it up and it has been a few months or years does not mean that you have been delivered from it. The Lord wants you delivered and not just practicing abstinence. There is a difference! When you are delivered, the soul tie is cut. I like to use the term cauterized. There is no possibility of the ends ever being put back together. If you are practicing abstinence, and you were a cigarette smoker, chances are you will go right back once you get around people who smoke. When you are in the company of other smokers and they offer you a cigarette, it will be harder to say, No! I know this to be true because I use to be the same way before the Lord delivered me, even if I had not smoked in six months. I hope that you catch what I am saying. I can remember smoking cigarettes over 20 years ago and had tried to quit several times on my own. I somehow kept going back to the same habit. I used every medical device the doctor prescribed. Nicotine patches, sprays, gum, and pills, but nothing seem to work. I had started smoking when I was about 16 years old. My mother and father smoked. It wasn't until the Lord saved me that shortly after being saved he delivered me from smoking. I can honestly say, that I never smoked another cigarette. It was so miraculous that he even took away the residue and I had no desire. I had been praying about it for a long time, but when I really got serious – things started happening. I threw away the ashtrays, cigarette lighters and even threw out the pack of cigarettes. The old folk use to call it cold turkey. It was hard at first, every time my soul and body told me that they wanted to smoke. I would say, "No, you're not getting another cigarette! I remember asking the Lord why I could not stop smoking before. He said "you enjoyed smoking". He said that I like the taste, and I enjoyed everything else that comes along with the feeling of smoking because I was addicted. I had never heard such a thing, but it resonated in my spirit. Oh, so that's why people keep doing certain things even when they know it's wrong because they enjoy it! And sin is pleasurable for season. God will never deliver you from anything that you enjoy doing. You must get to a place that you hate the very act.

⁂

Leaving that place, Jesus withdrew to the region of Tyre and Sidon. A Canaanite woman from that vicinity came to him, crying out. "Lord, Son of David, have mercy on me! My daughter is suffering terribly from demon- possession." Jesus did not answer a word. So, his disciples came to him and urged him, "Send her away, for she keeps crying out after us." He answered, "I was sent only to the lost sheep of Israel." The woman came and knelt before him, "Lord, help me!" she asked. He replied, "It is not right to take the children's bread and toss it to their dogs." "Yes Lord," she said, "but even the dogs eat the crumbs from the masters' table. Then Jesus answered, "Woman, you have great faith! Your request is granted." And her daughter was healed from that very hour. (Matthew 15:21- 28 NIV)

⁂

Deliverance is not a popular topic in many churches and while many churches shun or fail to mention deliverance, most of the new testament talks about it. Jesus healed the sick and feed the hungry, but he also cast out demons which is deliverance. It is not enough just to have salvation, you must be delivered to walk in total victory. Deliverance is not being preoccupied with demonic presence that consumes you, but it is being aware that it does exist.

Obedience is one of the keys to deliverance because is the act of complying with or submitting to a command, law or duty. When we follow the laws, commands, statues and precepts that God has put in place for us with our whole heart, chains will just begin to fall off little by little. If what I believe that God has said to be true, then my response to Him in faith is my obedience, therefore I have total trust that He will do just what he said. Jesus told the disciples.

"If you love me, you will obey what I command (John 14:15 NIV)

Obedience brings transformation and brings the Power of God into your life. There will be radical change when we begin to love Him from a pure heart with pure motives and intents, and not out of duty or obligation just for the sake of keeping the commandment. Obedience is mentioned in the bible more than

75 times and is a powerful weapon against the enemy. The enemy cannot overpower you when you are walking in obedience. He can try, but it will not work.

Prince of the power of the air is working in the sons of disobedience. It is the Spirit of God working in the lives of those that are obedient. When the enemy comes, you will not have anything in common with him, therefore he cannot over power you. Deliverance is the children's bread, but disobedience can delay your deliverance. Partial obedience is still disobedience which is as witchcraft. God cannot turn a blind eye to sin. Yes, He loves you, but sin stinks in the nostrils of God. God's promise is true to Abraham's descendants by faith which are those who believes in his son and those who do the will of the father. If you have received Christ as your savior and He is the Lord of your life, deliverance is now your birthright. There are a lot of things that we need deliverance from and the number one hindrance to deliverance is "self". I have found it to be true in my own experience that you really cannot sit at the feet and be taught of Him until You are delivered. Deliverance will help you with your broken focus because deliverance brings peace and clarity. You are more focused, your mind is sober, there is no hindrances that is stopping you from receiving the word. God wants you healed, delivered and set free in every area of your life. People who have been set free can never forget their deliverance. God does not want you to ever forget either. When

God delivered his people and took them over the Jordan Rivers, that was one of the first things he said to them once "they crossed over". So, I am telling you, if God has delivered you from anything, he wants that Jordan river experience in your life to be your testimony.

⚜

When the whole nation had finished crossing the Jordan, the Lord said to Joshua, "Choose twelve men from among the people, one from each tribe, and tell them to take up twelve stones from the middle of the Jordan from right where the priest stood and to carry them over with you and put them down at the place where you stay tonight." So, Joshua called together the twelve men he had appointed from the Israelites, one from each tribe, and said to them, Go over before the ark of the Lord your God into the middle of the Jordan. Each of you is to take up a stone on his shoulder, according to the number of tribes of the Israelites, to serve as a sign among you. In the future when your children ask you, "what do these stone mean?" tell them that the flow of the Jordan was cut off before the ark of the covenant of the Lord. When it crossed the Jordan, the waters of the Jordan were cut off. These stones are to be a memorial to the people of Israel forever." (Joshua 4: 1-7 NIV)

⚜

There are a lot of things that you need to be delivered from. I had things in me that I never knew existed. Sometimes I was so caught off guard by an obnoxious thought that I would have to repent for. I would have to tell the Lord, "I am sorry, that is not my thought". The Holy Spirit would say, "yes, it is". And would tell me the root of the thought. See, I was saved, but not yet delivered. I started seeing all kinds idiosyncrasies. The Holy Spirit would point out certain things during prayer time and give me strategies on how to overcome it. There were some things in my life that I wanted to give up but could not because I was addicted. No one likes to see themselves addicted, but am addiction is nothing more than a habit that you have formed which can be a physical or mental dependency on something or someone that has caused an obsession, devotion to, or passion for which causes you to incur adverse effects, or withdrawal when you either stop or go without this substance. Addiction is bondage and can be something so small as a cell phone, work, Facebook or even food. If there is anything in your life that you feel that you cannot go without - you are addicted and in need of deliverance. Deliverance in the Hebrew language (aphesis) means a release from bondage, imprisonment, etc. The kingdom of darkness which held you captive prior to receiving salvation wants to keep you in bondage which causes spiritual warfare. God will deliver you and bring you out with a strong hand just as he has done so many times before with the nation of Israel for He is a mighty deliverer. There is no power strong enough to stand up against the power of our God. Deliverance is your inheritance. God is calling you from the grave. That dark, cold secluded place that you have retreated to thinking it was a place of safety. You can put up walls to keep other from getting in, but at the same time it has become a cave for you. You have been there in that place so long that it will take Jesus to roll away the stone. Come out! and take off those grave clothes!

☙ ❧

They took away the stone. Then Jesus looked up and said, "Father, I thank you that you have heard me. "I knew that you always hear me, but I said this for the benefit of the people standing here, that they may believe that you sent me." When he had said this, Jesus called in a loud voice, "Lazarus, come out!" The dead man came out, his hands and feed wrapped with strips of linen, and a cloth around his face. Jesus said to them, "Take off the grave clothes and let him go." (John 11:41-44 NIV)

☙ ❧

Healing is your portion

It is not the will of God that you are sick. Sickness can be from the enemy or it could be the by-product from living in a fallen world. I do know that sickness can be an outward manifestation of what is going on inside of you spiritually. Did you know that a broken heart can manifest a certain illness? Bitterness and unforgiveness of soul can also manifest a certain illness. It is impossible to harbor bitterness, malice, strive and unforgiveness in your heart and pray to be healed. The enemy comes to steal,

59

kill and destroy because the enemy knows that your sickness will be a distraction to keep you from serving God. Most illness are associated with pain which not only affect you physically, but also emotionally and mentally. We are all too familiar with the story about Job Sickness is not always a result of sin, but it can be attributed to sin.

⁕⁕⁕

Job 2:6-9 The Lord said to Satan, "Very well, then, he is in your hands; but you must spare his life. So, Satan went out from the presence of the Lord and afflicted Job with painful sores from the soles of his feet t the top of his head. Then Job took a piece of broken pottery and scrapped himself with it as he sat among the ashes.

⁕⁕⁕

God allows the enemy to afflict your body because the righteous will sometimes suffer like the unrighteous, but God has not abandoned you. The bible declares that Job was blameless and upright and he was one who feared God, but still he was afflicted. There are some illnesses and sickness that you have allowed to enter due to your sin, or there could be sin through in your bloodline that has setup a generational curse. Gluttony is one of the biggest problems in the body of Christ because most of us are not as attentive to our bodies. We are not mindful of our over eating and weight gain causes our bodies to lack the proper nutrients that is needed to sustain us. The health issues that you see in the secular world is now plaguing the church it has been noted that the US is has the highest obesity rate in the world. There are some illnesses that we cause upon ourselves by damaging our bodies from prolonged use of medication, over eating and so forth, but God is still a healer. He has never lost his power to heal.

I conducted a case study using discernment on an individual in the work place setting a few year ago. The data was collected through conversation and observation. I chose this individual because she was a Christian and had health issues. For the sake of the case study, I changed her name to protect her identity. We will call her "Peaches", she is a very sweet Christian middle-aged woman. She has been with the company for ten years or more. She along with her husband and children all serve in the same church for more than twenty-five years. When I asked her how long she have been at the church, she smile and replied "I raised my children in that church". Peaches and I were always sharing our faith and discussing the Bible or a Christian song that we have heard during the week. Peaches had been having some ongoing health issues that she openly discusses with anyone who will listen and is currently on a lot of medication. A couple of months ago Peaches expressed to me that she has been having problems with her stomach and stated the Holy Spirit was nudging her to make an appointment with her physician, which she prolonged. One morning, her and I was talking and

I asked her how she was feeling and she told me that she finally got in to see the physician and I was excited to hear that. When I asked her, what did the doctor say, she replied "God, gave me Diverticulitis and Cholecystitis because I did not go to the doctor when the Holy Spirit told me to". I looked at her and said "God did not give you that illness". I discerned four key problems with her.

1. She thought her disobedience from not going to the doctor when she was first prompted by the Holy Spirit was a punishment from God, therefore I discerned fear and judgment.

2. She is an unbelieving believer. Due to her lack of faith she does not believe God for a healing. There are other family members in her immediate family sick. Her husband, her children, her grandchildren and her mother. I discern that she has not encounter anyone sick that has ever been healed by the Power of Jesus Chris, therefore she thinks that infirmity is the normal way of life.

3. Her church does not focus or teach on healing.

4. Lack of knowledge on her part, she thinks that healing has ceased and it was for the bible days, but not for today.

There are several possible solutions such as: share my faith, belief and testimony with her because I have been miraculously healed from a crippling condition that I suffered with for more than ten years. I was like the woman with the issue of blood in the bible who had gone to more than ten doctors and was taking a lot of medications that were causing other issues with my health, but no one could seem to help me. I can encourage her to get healing scripture and decree them over herself daily along with recommending a daily devotional or a book on Healing to build her faith. The best solution is prayer because it will take the power of the Holy Spirit to reveal to her by the stripes of Jesus we "are" healed.

꩜

But He was pierced for our transgressions, he was crushed for our iniquities; the punishment that us peace was upon him, and by his wounds we are healed. (Isaiah 53:5 NIV)

꩜

There are no benefits to you being sick, it is a limitation that hinders your walk with Christ. There are so many illnesses in the world today that not only affect your body, but also affect the entire well being of a person. You probably know someone sick or perhaps you are sick. You do not have to stay that way because God wants to heal you. If you are a disciple of Jesus Christ, you have the same power and authority in you to be healed and see others healed, but healing is in God's timing not yours.

Jesus called together his twelve disciples. He gave them authority to cast out evil spirits and to heal every kind of disease and illness. (Mat 10:1 NLT)

It does not matter how old you are. To God all sickness is the same and he can still heal cancer today like he can heal a common cold. He healed king Abimelech, his wife and slaves in Genesis 20:17-18 from barrenness. He healed Miriam, which was Aaron and Moses sister from leprosy in Number 12:10-15 after they complained about Moses marring a Cushite woman. He also healed Naaman from leprosy in II Kings 5:14. I love the story of Naaman being healed because he was a great man, commander of the army of a king, but he was a leper. Leprosy back then and even today is one of the most contagious and debilitating diseases. If you had leprosy, you were put outside of the camp away from family and friends.

"The person with such infectious disease must wear torn clothes, let his hair be unkept, cover the lower part of his face and cry out, Unclean, Unclean! as long as he has the infection he remains unclean. He must live alone; he must live outside the camp. (Lev 13:45-46 NIV)

Can you imagine how devastating it would be and the emotional wounds left by this disease. Leprosy was in a class all by itself. It was one of those "if God does not heal me, I will die" diseases. People back then died from leprosy because it was uncurable. I praise God for medical advancement, technology and scientific research which have afforded people longer life who suffer from immunodeficiency illnesses. People are living twenty and thirty years after being diagnosed. So, yes God is still a healer and you can be healed today! Healing is not just for yesterday. We must understand that the intent of the Father's healing is for you to advance the kingdom, not to sit home on the couch watching the soup opera. He wants his healing to be your testimony and how it changed your life and has caused you to love him in a deeper way. It is the will of the Father that you be healed. When we get sick, we pray "if it's your will". We really need to stop praying like that because it is his will to heal you. You need to pray "according to your will, but you cannot claim the promises to be healed if you do not know what they are. Healing is an act of Gods grace and forgiveness. The word "sozo" means to save and is translated by the verb "to heal" or to make whole which is the idea of saving from disease and its effects.

I have all sorts of journals that I keep for different reasons. I keep a separate journal that I called a "prayer journal" this book was more precious to me than any of the other journals because the only thing that I would write in this journal was prayer request for people, names of churches, pastors, and leader. I would list anyone that the Holy Spirit placed on my heart during prayer that needed divine intervention. When I first got saved and started reading the bible, I literally started taking God at his word. If his word says that "he will", then I was going to stand on that promise until "he does" I was always excited about what God was doing so I began to believe God for healing. I pulled these out of my prayer journal so that you could see the miracles.

January of 2011, I received a call from one of my sisters who was crying, scared and distraught. I could barely make out what she was saying. When I finally calmed her down to find out what happened, as she began to tell me. She said, "I went to bed feeling fine. When I woke up the left side of her face was twisted, speech was slurred and I cannot hear out of my left ear". She later went to the doctor and found out she did not have a stroke but she had something called Bell's Palsy. This is where the nerves in the muscle on one side of your face become paralyzed and it is very painful. I was not familiar with Bell's Palsy and had never heard of it, but she wanted me to pray that she would be healed. I prayed the prayer of faith over her and picked her up for church that week and the Bishop and his wife prayed the prayer of faith over her. Well, Feb 26, 2011 I got a call from my sister who said "My face is straighten back out". She had received most of the hearing back in her hear, but it was causing ringing in the ears. Praise God! I want you to see the time that it took God to heal her.

March 3, 2011, I got a call from a lady at the church who had slipped and fell on the ice due to a harsh winter. She went and had an MRI done and found out that she had a fractured tailbone and wrist. She was in so much paid and starting to get discouraged. I prayed the prayer of faith and God healed her miraculously. I was so confident that God would heal her that I did not wait for her to call me back with a praise report. I called her back on April 11 to see how she was feeling. I could not believe that it was the same person from a few days ago. She was joyous and excited, she said she was healed and the pain was gone. Glory to God!

Another one of my sisters was diagnosed with spinal meningitis in 2011 and was in and out of the hospital for months. This disease was fatal causing her to have surgery on her brain, she had memory loss and she lost the activity of all her motor skills. She had to learn how to walk and talk again. She could do nothing for herself. I remember showing up at the hospital and asking the doctor about her conditions. I remember the doctor talking with me in the family room at the hospital as she began to whisper. She said "There is nothing else that we can do for your sister, she will always have the mind of a three-year old". I was so shocked at how fast things were spiraling out of control.

I prayed for my sister every day. Not only did I pray for her, but I packed up all my stuff and moved to Georgia and stayed with her and her husband and help to care for her until she got better. God has healed her body. The doctors are still amazed at her recovery. My sister is saved and serving the Lord with everything he has. God is the same today, yesterday and forever more. There is a story in the bible about a man named Elijah and how he prayed that it would not rain and the bible said "at the word of his mouth" it did not rain. Prayer is powerful when you use it.

❦

If you are sick, ask the church leaders to come and pray for you. Ask them to put olive oil on you in the name of the Lord. If you have faith when you pray for sick people, they will get well. The Lord will heal them, and if they have sinned, he will forgive them. If you have sinned, you should tell each other what you have done. Then you can pray for one another and he healed. The prayer of an innocent person is powerful, and it can help a lot. (James 4:14-16 CEV)

❦

CHAPTER FOUR
The Clash of two kingdoms

Light & Darkness

There is the kingdom of light and the kingdom of darkness which is a continuous fight between good and evil. There is an enemy that is waging spiritual war against you for your soul based on what Jesus has done on the cross. Spiritual means you are warring against a spirit of invisibility and power. A supernatural being without a material body, such as an angel, demon. Not earthly or sensual, in fact spiritual is an after-Pentecost word used in the New Testament.

Supernatural is anything that exist or occur beyond the known forces of nature that are believed to be demons, or other agents unconstrained by natural law. They are bodiless, and nonphysical. Satan was an angel and he was expelled from heaven and one third of the angles followed him. This is the enemies you should want to know about and what he is doing.

Spiritual beings must take on a body to be legal on the earth. God came to earth in a body which was Jesus when he took on the form of a human. Satan used the body of the serpent in the garden to influence Eve. The enemy is battling for your soul because he wants to control or influence your mind, your will and emotions.

You are in a battle every day, whether you are sleeping or awake. The Bible is full of war stories, from the beginning with the first mention of war between the seed of the serpent and the seed of the woman in the book of Genesis. The war is not just against the woman, but against her seed. The seed of righteousness warring against the seed of unrighteousness. The seed of righteousness would be the heir or decedents of Abraham by faith and the unrighteous would be the children of disobedience.

C୰ఇ෯

So, the Lord God said to the serpent, "Because you have done this, cursed are you above all the livestock and all the wild animals! You will crawl on your belly and you will eat dt all the days of your life. And I will put enmity between you and the woman, and between your offspring and hers; he will crush your head and you will strike his heel." and her seed; it shall bruise thy head and thou shall bruise his heel. (Genesis 3: 14-15 NIV)

C୰ఇ෯

Abraham had to fight to help rescue Lot, his nephew when he was taken captive, the bible says that Abraham and three hundred and eighteen members from his household fought against the five kings to rescue Lot. Joshua fought against the Amalekites, and Gideon fight against the Midianites.

Throughout the history of time, there have always been a nation that came up to war against the children of Israel. Wars that are fought is almost always over land or territory with the primary intent being ownership. David fought against the Philistines when he was a young boy and he killed Goliath, but that did not stop the enemy. You would have thought that the Philistines would have retreated and that you would never hear from them again. Not so, when David was appointed as the king of Israel more than twenty years later, he still had to fight the Philistines. Spiritual warfare is real just like you have lungs, kidneys and a spleen that you have not seen with your natural eye, but you are confident that you have them. So why is it so hard for people, especially Christians to believe that there is an arch enemy that is warring against your mind, your children, your marriage, your finances, your health, your business, and even your ministry. Everything that God says is yours, he wants it and will stop at nothing until he gets it. There is a continuous strong opposition against the church such as violence, hatred, oppression along with other kinds of unimaginable evil.

In Some countries outside of the United States people are being tortured, burned and even killed for professing Christ as their savior. There are some churches that have gone underground, such as in China where people started meeting in homes and has branched out into smaller groups due to fear of being arrested because they are an unregistered church and they face punishment for operating outside of a legal institution. It is not the will of God that people are oppressed by governmental systems. In the old testament, God heard the cries of His people and delivered them. He will hear you and deliver you. His arm is not short that He cannot save you nor is His ear dull that He cannot hear you. The enemy is constantly plotting a demise to hinder the plans and purpose of God in your life, and one of the greatest weapons that the enemy use is discouragement. It does not matter how smart, beautiful, powerful, strong or rich you are. The plan of the enemy is to get you to think contrary to what the word says, then most likely you will become discouraged and feel defeated which eventually will cause you to slow down, and then inevitably stop the work. I have been there, there have been times and seasons in my life that I have felt so defeated and wanted to give up, exhausted and overwhelmed. I thank God for that driving force (Holy Ghost) on the inside that would not let me quit. This force is greater than anything on the earth. There is no power greater than the Holy Ghost power. If there was not an invisible world that reaches far beyond what your natural eye could see, I don't think Paul would be telling the Ephesians how to prepare to battle this unseen force.

⟨⟩

Finally, my brethren be strong in the Lords and in his mighty power. Put on the full armor of God so that you can take your stand against the devil's' schemes. For our struggle is not against flesh and blood, but against the rulers, against the authorities, against the powers of this dark world and against the spiritual forces of evil in the heavenly realms. Therefore, put on the full armor of God, so that when the day of evil comes, you may be able to stand your ground, and after you have done everything, to stand (Ephesians 6:10-13 NIV)

⟨⟩

There is a rivalry between God's kingdom which is the kingdom of light and Satan's kingdom which is the kingdom of darkness. A rival is a competitor or opponent, challenger or adversary who tries to get what only one can have. The objective is to wrestle you for it with hand to hand combat, pin you down and take it by force. In the book of Ephesians Paul was equipping and encouraging the new believers that now they have received salvation, they have been drafted into God's army. Like a natural army that has a commander in chief, armor and artillery is required to win the war. You must wear the armor for your protection and use the weapons provided to win.

Paul said "Finally" which is not a word you hear often but is of great importance. In other words, after you have done everything that you have known to do, after you have come through a long and difficult time, *"be strong in the Lord and in the power of His might"*. There are some things on this Christian journey that seem like it will never end. I have had a lot of days where I thought," how long Lord". You must make sure you are following the process prescribed in the bible and not some new Idea that you came up with. I don't care how long it takes, you will get victory over it. It is not your war so you do not have to be afraid, intimidated or feel inadequate in your own strength because the victory belongs to the Lord. Yes, it may get hard and yes you may become weary at times which is only a natural reaction to all mankind. There is nothing wrong with being a Christian and getting weary, just don't stay weary. The Lord knows when you feel defeated. Look at Joshua, God had to encourage him so many times.

⁕

Be strong and courageous, because you will lead these people to inherit the land I swore to their forefathers to give them. Be strong and very courageous. Be careful to obey all the law my servant Moses gave to you; do not turn from it to the right or left, that you may be successful wherever you go. Do not let this book of the law depart from your mouth; meditate on it day and night, so that you may be careful to do everything written in it., Then you will be prosperous and successful. Have not I commanded you? Be strong and courageous. Do not be terrified; do not be discouraged, for the Lord your God will be with you wherever you go." (Joshua 1: 6-9 NIV)

C&8833D

When you are following the ways of the Lord, the Holy Spirit raises a standard against the enemy concerning you and a host of angels are waring on your behalf. Throughout the bible, God always used ministering angels to encourage, console and proclaim the word of the Lord over people lives. When Elijah was running from Jezebel and he became afraid and weary in 1 Kings 19; God sent an angel to minister to him. It was during that time that the angel touched Elijah and told him to eat because the journey ahead is too great. To win the war, you must be submitted in every area of your life to the Lord. Once you realize that you are plugged in to the power source, the battle is over. You will not run another day in your life. It was only when Moses hands were lifted (which is a sign of surrender- to give up completely) Amalek did not prevail against the children of God. When Moses put his hands down, Amalek prevailed. The running is over, you must face life's circumstance head on. It is alright to get angry with the devil and let him know that you will not be backed into a corner. He is hostile and relentless toward you. I looked back over my life at the things the enemy had influenced or persuaded me to do, so I decided I will not stand by passively and let him wreak havoc on my life or the lives of others. He will not let up until you exercise your authority. It is only when we Learn to rely on the Lord, that our enemy is defeated. Wrestling is one of the oldest combat sports today that is competitive with two opponents doing hand-to-hand combat that was later developed by Ancient Greek to train soldiers. Wrestling is still a well-known sport and is still being used today in many other countries. In your spiritual wrestling match, it is not against flesh and blood, but you are wrestling or warring against persons without bodies. Paul not only described the armor that you need to put on, but also what you are fighting against. When you are given a task to do, you are usually given the tools you need to accomplish the job.

This is the armor of the Lord, so it has already been tested, tried and proven. It is encouraging to know that God has already tested the armor himself and he knows that it works. It is only when we put His armor on that we are undefeated. Helmet of salvation which guards the head, sober thinking, knowledge of truth along with having the mind of Christ. Notice the importance of the helmet that protect the head. David was a warrior and he knew the secret, if he could give a fatal blow to Goliath head, the rest of the body would crumble. If the enemy can distort your thinking he knows it won't be long before your thoughts will become your actions. Something that you must do is to take authority over our mind and you decide what thoughts you will not entertain. Thinking is a part of your human nature and it is an attribute of God. When you got born again, you received a new spirit, not a new body so now your spirit that wants to please God is warring with your mind. That is why the bible tells you to "put on the mind of Christ because your mind is a battlefield. When you have the mind of Christ, nothing is impossible with God. Your mind just does not automatically change once you are born again, I wish it was that easy. Your emotions do not change overnight, you will still crave and desire the things that once pleased you until we learn how to put our flesh under subjection, which is not an easy task. When you are born again you have the Spirit of God living in you, it will illuminate old habits, old mind set, old life styles, and it will begin to tear those ideologies down, but it will not happen all at once. You will start to notice some subtle changes. You always get thoughts that come to your mind, whether good or bad, but you should be thinking about positive things, things that are praiseworthy, admirable, lovely, and think on those things that are truthful. It is the thoughts that you meditate on that will shape your future. You have the power to decide what thoughts you will keep and which ones you will discard.

A stronghold is a fortress or a fortified place. A place that has military strength. A stronghold or fortress can be natural or spiritual. A spiritual stronghold can be a thought, a belief system or false doctrine set up in your mind that have been there over long periods of time that causes you to react to certain situations. The enemy will always speak totally opposite of what the word says, that is why Jesus used the word of God as a spiritual weapon to refute his lies. The lies from the enemy are always words of defeat like: your child will never be saved, your marriage will never survive, women should not preach, you cannot afford the house, you will never go back to school, you do not qualify for that job, you will never make it out alive, or most people die from that disease. Lie after lie, after lie.

When truth comes, it is likened to a battering ram that is pounding against that belief system to tear it down.

It will take the Holy Spirit to pull down that fortified mind set. When the enemy set up a stronghold in your mind it acts as a city or community under siege that is being held captive. The city has high walls and is surrounded by a gate and bars which have gatekeepers at the gate to monitor activity. Gates represent access because gates can keep you in or out. In the old Testament there was always transaction, exchanges, business deals going on at the city gate. This is where elders and leaders sat and laws were passed. The enemy is so cunning, your stronghold may be so easily dismissed that it goes by undetected. There are things that you were taught as a young child that you are still doing today and don't know why. It could be something so simple as to what you have learned in school as a preschooler, something a neighbor said, or your mother or father has instilled in you at a young age. There is a certain thought pattern instilled in you either by the educational system, society or ministry that governs your actions. It is a reinforced thought pattern, belief system, or ideology that is strong. This is something that have been built up over time that is so strong that it causes confusion of the mind and can cause some to fall away from the faith. There is still is a remnant that is still standing in faith. Recognize thought patterns which can be damaging that come from the enemy to alter your destiny.

Check every thought against the word because when you meditate on things that are not true, your mind stores the thought subconsciously to be used against you later. Your mind is like a filing cabinet full of old files and every thought the comes to your mind, it unlocks your mental filing cabinet and it began to check your mental files looking for another thought that you have ever had that is exactly like it. Your mind is looking for a similar thought that you had and what reaction, response or outcome did you experience. When I gained this revelation, it opened a whole new world. The more you meditate in the Word of God, the more your thoughts are replaced with the Word of God, the enemy will never have anything to compare that thought to.

❧❦❧

Jesus said to them, "If God were your father, you would love me, for I came from God and now am here. I have not come on my own; but he sent me. Why is my language not clear to you? Because you are unable to hear what I say. You belong to your father, the devil, and you want to carry out your father's desire. He was a murderer from the beginning not holding to the truth, for there is no truth in him. When he lies, he speaks his native language, for he is a liar and the father of lies. Yet because I tell you the truth, you do not believe me! (John 8:42-45 NIV)

❧❦❧

The second piece of armor is the breast plate of righteousness which guards your chest area which incases your heart. The heart is the very core of your being. The bible says that David was a man after God's own heart.

God is pure and holy, there is no shadow of turning in Him. His motives toward his children are always good, of pure intent, not shifting or changing. If your heart is pure then your actions will be pure. If your heart is deceitful, so will your actions be. Everything we do and every word that we speak come from what is in our hearts. Our actions are just an outward manifestation of what is in the heart. Your heart is the real you, the inner person. If your heart is clean(pure) then your eyes will be pure, your ears will be pure, and your speech will be pure. The word heart is used several times in scripture, I believe because natural man cannot live without a heart, it is the essence of human life. It is the centering of everything in your body because every vital organ in the body depends on the heart. God created the body with a heart to pump the blood throughout the body, to supply the organ with oxygen and remove waste. Christ should be our heartbeat for every task you take on, every assignment given, every mission you embark upon. He is your life source the very essence of your being and literally you cannot live without Him. When the hearts stop beating, it will not be long before the organs of the body began to stop functioning like the kidneys, liver, brain, and lungs. Christ redeemed us by the precious shedding of his blood, he gave his life for the world because of his love for mankind.

You also have the belt of truth, the shield of faith, shoes shod with peace and the sword of the Spirit. I am not going to spend time on all the pieces of armor, but the most important thing to walk away with is that God has provided you with protection. All these pieces of armor are the same armor that a combat soldier use today. When I think about my supernatural weapons I name three major weapons, in this order: Weapon#1 -The Word, because is silences the enemy. Weapon#2 – Prayer because it stops the enemy. Weapon#3 – Praise, because it confuses the enemy. A natural war is fought with natural artillery such as guns, knives, arrows, rockets, missiles, chemical and biological weapons.

Paul was encouraging the Ephesians to be strong. A riot broke out and there was a lot of controversy about Pauls' teachings about this one true God because the people in Ephesus had been worshipping Artemis and to be told that Artemis is not a god stirred up a lot of wrath. This church was facing a lot of opposition and hardship for the sake of the gospel. Paul wanted to make sure that they did not become weary in well doing after all they have been taught, all the preaching he had done. Paul wanted to make they stay the course until Christ is formed in them. The end conclusion is this "be strong, do not faint, do not become weary and loose heart. God is going to come through in a mighty way. Rely on the strength of the Lord because in our strength we can do nothing. Acknowledge that the power in you comes from the Lord. It is the Lord fighting for you, and through you and you will get the victory over the enemy. Spiritual warfare is like carbon monoxide, yo8u can not see if, but it is deadly. You cannot see gas leaking, but it is deadly. When I plug in my coffee pot, I cannot see the electricity flowing through the outlet but it is real.

There are many forms of spiritual warfare that the enemy launch against the children of God to immobilize and restrict your movement. Oppression and depression is a form of spiritual warfare that we most often war against and it has risen to new heights, not only in the secular world but even in the church. The enemy infiltrate your mind with words and imagery to refute the word of God and to defame the character and identity of who God says you are. Oppression is when you feel weighed down in body or mind, and it causes you to feel overwhelmed, tormented, sad or defeated. It can cause you to feel afraid, hopeless, and in despair. Most people who suffer from panic attacks maybe caused by oppression. This is a spirit that comes upon a person, it is not the person conjuring up this emotional state of being, but it comes to paralyze you and to keep you in stagnant position which hinders the believer from living out your full potential in God. It is like a procrastinator who has a desire to do things of God but has a delay in doing them. The enemy knows if he can keep you putting things off until tomorrow, you will never do it. In fact, you are moving further and further away from your desired goal. If you live a defeated life you will never reach your God given destiny. Normally depression and oppression are terms you may hear used simultaneously because they somewhat similar, but different.

❦

And you know that God anointed Jesus of Nazareth with the Holy Spirit and with Power. Then Jesus went around doing good and healing all who were oppressed by the devil, for God was with him. (Acts10:38 NLT)

❦

Oppression happens externally. The enemy knows if you are experiencing defeat, and uncertainty he does not have to worry about you using your authority as a Christian to subdue him or his activity. It is time the enemy is "unmasked" and that you see him for who he really is. The Lord does not want you oppressed and the bible tells you to take off the spirit of heaviness and put on the garment of praise and that God may be glorified. You consciously need to do something. You have to take it off! Tell the enemy that does not belong to you. The Holy Spirit showed me a sign to watch out for a couple of years ago because I suffered oppression and depression at the hands of the enemy for many years. I did not know much about either condition at that time, but I knew something was wrong and I felt I had no control over it or it or how to stop it. After the Lord healed my thought and emotions, he helped me to recognized the thoughts when they come back.

Whenever there is a voice in your head speaking in a third-person, that is the enemy. Let me make it clear. If you get a thought that says to you "what you need to do is". That is not the Holy Spirit. Depression is internally and more severe than oppression, although it is hard to differentiate between the two. Depression is treatable in one of two ways by medication prescribed by a physician or through a deliverance session. People who are in deep depression normally always have suicidal thoughts and some lead to suicide which is always the end results. If oppression is not dealt with, it will lead to depression and can cause harm to others and self. This is a topic no one wants to talk about in the church. Through research, I found that depression can be traced back to sin in your life perhaps caused by a traumatic experience and most of the time it is secret sin. I have been delivered from depression but looking back I know that to be true. This traumatic experience opened the door to other sins that caused bondage. God's word confirms His plans for your life in scripture and it is the same scripture that God is speaking over your life even today. God sees you healed, whole, joyous, full of life, wealthy and wise. God see you opposite of the way the world sees you and even the way you see yourself. He sees you living above and not beneath, being a lender and not a borrower. Living in the overflow financially, spiritually and physically. God sees you prospering in every area of your life. For *I know the plans I have for you, saith the Lord. They are plans of good and not of disaster, to give you a hope and a future. (Jeremiah 29:11 NLT)*

CHAPTER FIVE
Nothing can hold you back

Self is the is the biggest hinderance

You were created with unlimited potential to soar above every situation, and circumstance. There are things in your life that keeps you from soaring and reaching your full potential such as old mind sets, habits, hang-up, generational curses, addictions, anger, bitterness, unforgiving heart, soul ties, malice, strife and that is just to name a few. The list is continuous and goes on and on.

There are things in you that are manifesting now or even in the lives of your children or grandchildren because of the life you lived before you surrendered your life to Christ because sin has consequences. Some things you have done, some things were passed down from your parents and ancestors going back to the fourth and fifth generation that is holding you back from serving God in a greater capacity. The Almighty God wants to break the power of the enemy over your life today and remove the Egypt mentality from your mind. God used Moses to free the Israelites from Egypt, Egypt was Instilled in the minds of the people. All they could think about was going back to Egypt because they had been there so long, that was all they knew. They had gotten to a point that every time something would happen, they wanted to go back. There was nothing good in Egypt. The Israelites were slaves, they had been beaten, treated unfairly, demoralized, and the given rigorous work to do. I cannot believe that was the life they always talked about going back to. I am quite sure when they were in Egypt they probably talked about one day being free. Have you ever been in a dangerous situation or maybe abusive relationship and God opened a door of escape where he takes away fear and give you courage. You may have wanted to leave many times before but could not bring yourself to do it, to leave. By the grace of God, you got out on your own and God supernaturally supplies all your needs. As you began the healing and restoration phase in your life, a few months have gone by and you are doing pretty good and making great strides, but out of nowhere you begin to think about the life you use to have. The enemy begin to replace his thoughts with your thoughts and before long you are thinking "things were not really that bad in Egypt". Once that thought is there, your emotions attach themselves and now you are desiring to be there.

This is a good time to be praying and calling out to God because if he has the power to save and deliver you from a situation – He has the power to keep you. The Israelites old mentality consumed their new life and kept them in the desert for forty years when they should have been moving forward. God's promise is for you, your children and grandchildren. In the book of Joshua, the people could not image passing over the Jordan river. God spoke to Joshua and had him to tell the people "get ready because in three days they are crossing the Jordan". God had to reassure Joshua that once they moved out in faith, then he would cut off the water. That scripture is a confidence builder. He did not say "after everyone gets in". He did not say "after you are half way across". He did not say "When I see that you are drowning" then he was going to move on their behalf. Read the scripture aloud

And it shall come to pass, as soon as the soles of the feet of the priests that bear the ark of the Lord, the Lord of all the earth, shall rest in the waters of Jordan, that the waters of Jordan shall be cut off from the waters that come down from above; and they shall stand upon a heap. (Joshua 3:13 NKJV)

The Lord said "when the soles of the feet". That means God is watching and when the Priest (those that have been consecrated unto God) pick up your feet and make an attempt to cross over, that he will do the rest. Some people would rather stay in bondage than to trust God because it is easier and it does not cost them anything. A life of uncertainty is bondage because God has proven himself to be credible, time and time again The Israelites were free physically, but mentally they were still enslaved or in bondage. There are a lot of people who look free on the outside but are in chains and shackles in their mind. Mental bondage is when the reality of who you are is so weaken that you take on the personality of someone that you are not. The Lord showed me a powerful example of what bondage looks like in the life of a believer and a non- believer and the difference between possession and oppression. It is like a house for Sale verses a house for Rent. If you have ever looked for a place to live and you saw an advertisement in the yard "for rent" or "for sale" you knew which criteria you were looking for. A non-believer can experience demonic possession which is where he or she is completely controlled by another force that drives them to murder, steal, commit sexual immorality and every unimaginable act against their neighbor. When you are full of darkness and there is no light in you, you are controlled by darkness giving the demonic forces legal rights to take up habitation. They consider the body that they have inhabited as their home and that person have no input or authority to stop or evict them. We talked about depression earlier and it is classified as a psychological state of being; low in spirit and is normally treated by medication. On the other hand, a born-again believer cannot be possessed, but you can be oppressed, tormented or even harassed. If a person is sentenced to prison for a crime, once incarcerated you immediately lose your rights. You lose your dignity and your identity because you have been handed over to another who is the authoritative figure in their life. Prisoners are told what to do and when to do it. They do not have the option of disagreeing because there will be consequences. You basically have no choice because all your freedoms are taken away and you are confined and isolated from the outside world. Everyone in the prison system is being conformed to the same system.

Once the person is released from prison and placed back into society they will have to be trained how to function and interact in society as a citizen. Most of the rules and stipulation while serving time in prison is different than those outside of prison walls. A natural prison has bars, cells and tall barbwire fence with a sharp shooter in the tower that you can see with your natural eye. It is much harder to see spiritual possession or bondage because the bars are invisible and cannot be seen with the natural eye. There are some prisoners who risk their lives trying to break free, only to be apprehended and returned behind bars to face greater punishment for their failed attempt.

As a believer in the Lord Jesus Christ, on the other hand has the Holy Spirit living in your Spirit and you are sealed until the day of redemption. You can experience an unjust, cruel exercise of power or authority from an employer, government, law enforcement, etc. with means to crush by abuse; to be a burden to mentally or spiritually.

When I purchased my house I also became the proud owner of the land. I remember wanting to put up a privacy fence, but to make sure I was not on my neighbor's property I had to hire a land surveyor which came out and surveyed the land. The surveyor found the boundary lines and marked the four corners of the property by driving steel pegs in the ground. When I took possession of the house, I am not just owner of the house, but I now own everything in the house including the doors, windows, sink, cabinets and flooring. I have the liberty to change and update anything in the house as I choose without getting an approval from anyone else. I can change the drapes, the paint, or even change out the appliances. I can make drastic changes by adding an addition to the house, exterior painting, landscaping or putting in a swimming pool. I hope you are getting the picture. There is a tree in my front yard that is starting to lean toward the street, and because it is in my yard, I also own the tree and I am going to get it cut down this spring.

Jesus called them and spoke to them in parable: "How can Satan drive out Satan? If a kingdom is divided against itself, that kingdom cannot sand. If a house is divided against itself, that house can not stand and if Satan opposes himself and is divided, he cannot stand; his end has come. In fact, no one can enter a strong man's house and carry off his possessions unless he first ties up the strong man. Then he can rob his house. (Mark 3:23-27 NIV)

The enemy use to be the strong man in your life which kept you in bondage, but when you became a Christian, the Holy Ghost power has come to bind the strongman in your life and rob him of all his goods and serve him with an eviction. The enemy knows he can not possess you and he has no authority over you. He can certainly try to oppress you by frustrating you if you let him. He tried to do the same thing with Nehemiah when he heard that the wall of Jerusalem had been broken down and the gates had been burned with fire. The Lord put it on the heart of Nehemiah to go back and repair the city. There was opposition from the enemy to get him to stop the work. Most people will tell you "It don't take all of that" or "What are doing that for". It is to get you to slow down and stop the work of our Lord Jesus Christ.

When Sanballat heard that we were rebuilding the wall, he became very angry and was greatly incensed. He ridiculed the Jews, and in the presence of his associates and the army of Samaria, he said, "What are those feeble Jews doing? Will they restore their wall? Will they offer sacrifices? Will they finish in a day? Can they bring the stones back to life from those heaps of rubble — burned as they are? Tobiah the Ammonite, who was at his side, said, "What they are building — If even a fox climbed up on it, he would break down their wall of stone! (Nehemiah 4:1-3 NIV)

I remember being in prayer once and I was crying out to the Lord at the altar and in such a travail. Later, I heard someone say "you don't have to pray that loud because God is not hard of hearing". That was an attempt to stop the progress. They were correct in saying the God is not hard of hearing, but there are some scriptures that say shout to the Lord with a voice of triumph. The Lord was not hard of hearing when he told Joshua to march around the Jericho wall and "shout". Some walls in your life will not fall until you "shout". Not once did Nehemiah stop building the wall, day and night he worked until it was finally finished.

Whatever area in your life that you seem to struggling in is due to oppression from the enemy, God prevails even through opposition and adversity. It is easy for most Christians to acknowledge that sickness is from the enemy. They have a hard time acknowledging that the same enemy that comes to oppress or afflict your body through sickness is the same enemy that comes to oppress your soul (mind, will or emotions). Have you noticed in church when a person has a physical ailment or maybe on a crutch or in a wheelchair, people are more apt to call them to the altar, anoint them with oil and pray the prayer of faith. What happens to the person sitting there in the service who is being tormented in the mind and haunted by images of their past, nightmares, or thoughts of suicide that you cannot see. When was the last time you saw a person come in sick, bound by sin or an addiction and left changed by the Power of God? I heard a pastor preaching about how we have put the Holy Spirit in a box, metaphorically speaking. It's not a very big box more like a shoe box that we put our shoes in and place on the closet shelf. On Sunday mornings we put the box in the car and take it to church and put the box on the pew and take the top off at a certain time of service and say Go! Holy Spirit, you have 30 minutes to move on the congregation, reducing the Holy Spirit to a time restraint in which to work during an orchestrated service that is catered to man rather than to God. Most of the time they leave the same way they came because you could not spiritually discern that they are spiritually oppressed and need deliverance.

Jesus came to set the captive free. That's what he came for, so that you and I could be free. There were a lot of sick people in Jesus's day and most of them where in the synagogue (the synagogue being the church, the place of worship) They were bound by some type of infirmity and siting in the church. God's house shall be called a house of prayer. Why? Because it does not matter what you are bound by. This is the one place that he set up that you can go and be delivered. The woman with the infirmity was like that for eighteen years, but she kept coming to the church. Her infirmity was a debilitating disease because the bible says that she could in no way lift herself up. Like many today who continue to come to the church and leaving the same way because no one has the power to lose you from your infirmity. Choir members singing in the choir but bound. Praise and worship leaders, door keepers, altar workers, greeters, bible study teachers, praise dancers, and prayer team are bound, and no one has the power to lift you up. Some people shout and run abound the church like they are free until church is over. When they get home, they are still bound. Religion does not have the power to set you free because religion is nothing more than human idea or tradition with a Christian overtone. You can pray all night, use a whole bottle of extra virgin olive oil and put a dolly on your head all as a part of a religious act, but without faith it is impossible to please God. Religion cause you to go through the motion without getting real results. Religion is following a whole lot of rules. And we all know there is no power in that! That's why Jesus had to come because the children of God could not keep them and kept going after strange gods. Some people look religious but have no power! People are looking for the power like the bible says.

On the Sabbath day Jesus was teaching in one of the synagogues, and a woman was there who had been crippled by a spirit for eighteen years. She was bent over and could not straighten up at all. When Jesus saw her, he called her forward and said to her, "Woman, you are set free from your infirmity." Then he put his hands on her, and immediately she straightened up and praised God. (Luke 13:10-13 NIV)

I remember a friend of mine was a member of a church and invited me to a revival. She told me that her church does not believe in women wearing pants. I made sure that I put on a dress to honor their house when I went. When I got there, and as I looked around almost every lady in the church had on a long skirt down to the ankles. They wore no make up and all of them had their hair pulled back. I gathered that the ladies who had on pants or a skirt right below the knee where visitors. We sang song after song. They prayed and preached and sang. Then they testified and sang and sang and preached. It was dry! Just because you erect a building and call it a church does not mean that the Glory of the Lord is in that place. They did not sing with real conviction. To me being a first-time visitor, even their testimonies where dry and just empty words. You can tell when a church has fire! The atmosphere is different. There was no compassion about the Lord, or what he had done. Then things began to turn around rather quickly when this woman who was sitting down quietly with the "pants" on, got up and began to sing "Pass me not oh gently savior, hear my humbly cry", the Holy Spirt and the anointing began to fall in that place. I truly believe those who thought they were saved; got saved all over again. God wants to do something new and fresh, but he wants to do it. He does not want you to conjure it up like Nadab and Abihu, Aaron two son took their censers and put fire in them and added incense from the altar and offered it to the Lord on the altar. The movement of God is not stale and dry, you need the anointing because that is what makes the difference. You have gotten so accustomed to doing things a certain way and it is no longer working. Jesus was teaching in the synagogue and she was in the right place and the right time. She came to meet with God and receive divine direction. She knew if she could just get to the place where the presence of God dwells, where his Glory is resting and it is so tangible. Jesus was able to see that there was a spirit behind her illness causing a physical handicap, but once He spoke to her issue she was able to receive her healing.

The scripture says that she could in no way lift herself up. Today when we are sick, we try over the counter medication and old household remedies that have been in the family for years hoping it will work. Healthcare is so expensive which is usually the last resort, therefore most people seek medical advice only in cases of a true emergency. Even then there is no guarantee that you will feel better once you leave. Jesus wants to heal you so that you can work for the kingdom. Christians have the Holy Spirit living on the inside to empower them to do greater works for the kingdom and not to live a life unto oneself. The Bible makes it very clear that she has tried in her own efforts to free herself. Losing your health is a common fear among most people because it brings you to a place of helplessness. There is no health condition that is incurable. It does not matter how long you've had cancer, tumors, back condition or any other condition. Did you know that at the name of Jesus, sickness must bow its knee to the Great Physician?

⟡⟡⟡⟡⟡

And we know that in all things, God words for the good of those who love him, who have been called according to his purpose. (Roman 8:28 NIV)

⟡⟡⟡⟡⟡

Yes, even sickness is working for your good. It does not feel good, but there are some powerful testimonies how God confound the physicians because He is the great physician. Even through sickness we can learn to draw near to God and He will draw near to us. Have sweet fellowship and build a more intimate relationship with the Holy Spirit during that time. This is a time to cast your cares on Him, your worries, fears and insecurities on Him for He cares for you. You are predestined for greatness. I affirmed that I can do all things thru Christ who strengthen me because the greater one lives on the inside. You are valuable to the kingdom of God. Jesus ministry was short yet powerful, He fulfilled the law, called disciple and led them by example how to cast out demons and heal the sick which was His primary ministry.

A Blessed Life is a balanced life

God wants you to have balance in your life. In the Old and New Testament, it talks about mother and father which is an example of balance. The father as a firm, authoritative figure and then there is the mother being gentle as the nurturer. Jesus did not just heal, but he healed and cast out demons. This new age religion only wants to believe in healing and cast aside the casting out of demons as if it never happened. There is much talk about the kingdom of light, but not about the kingdom of darkness. There is a kingdom of darkness who afflict, torment, harass and compel you to sin. In this generation most people do not want to talk about demonic influence, but once you acknowledge that it does exist it exposes the enemy and shines the light on darkness. The ultimate mission of the kingdom of darkness is to keep you from knowing Christ which spiritual blindness is. It is like an alcoholic drinking every day, until you acknowledge that you have a drinking problem, you will never seek out help and will always be bound by alcoholism. When God set you free and deliver you from the kingdom of darkness into the kingdom of light it is to further the kingdom of God and so that you can be a beacon of light for someone. It is so you can reach back and pull someone else out of darkness. I kept trying to figure out why Jesus kept telling the people every time he would heal them he would say, "Go and sin no more." Many of the people throughout the bible who Jesus healed, he told to go and sin more unless something worse come upon you. What about the man beside the pool of Bethesda who set there thirty-eight years until one day he had an encounter with Jesus that changed his whole life.

⚜

Later, Jesus went to Jerusalem for another Jewish festival. In the city near the sheep gate was a pool with five porches, and its name in Hebrew was Bethzath. Many sick, blind, lame, and crippled people were lying close to the pool. Beside the pool was a man who had been sick for thirty-eight years. When Jesus saw the man and realized that he had been crippled for a long time, he asked him,

"Do you want to be healed?" The man answered, "Lord, I don't have anyone to put me in the pool when the water is stirred up. I try to get in, but someone else always gets there first. Jesus told him, "Pick up your mat and walk!" Right then the man was healed. He picked up his mat and started walking around. The day on which this happened was a Sabbath. (John 5:1-9 CEV)

Later, Jesus met the man in the temple and told him, "You are now well. But don't sin anymore or something worse might happen to you. (John 5:14 CEV)

You may not be totally aware of the power you have locked up on the inside waiting to change someone else's life. People walked by this man every day for thirty-eight years while he lay there with this same issues and problem. He had been there so long that the onlooker accepted it as normal because their senses were numbed. I can hear the man crying out just from me reading the story. People that you pass every day is crying out for help. These are the silent cries of the heart. If this man has been in this condition for thirty-eight years, Jesus is not the only person that should have recognized that he needed help. Jesus healed people everywhere he went because he could identify with their human frailty because he was human.

He knew that his assignment given by the father was given to him to transform their lives which entail restoring back to the original state of wholeness. If you have ever been broken and healed, you know what brokenness feels like and can identify with those that are broken. Jesus was wounded for you, so he knows what it feels like to be wounded.

CHAPTER SIX
The Bondage Breaker

Repentance brings Restoration

Repentance is necessary and it simply mean to have Godly sorrow for your sins, turn and go in an opposite direction. The Holy Spirit will not fight against anything that you are not fighting against. You will never be delivered and set free from anything that you Love. John the Baptist came preaching repentance, Jesus came preaching repentance and Peter preached the same message after his upper-room experience.

❦

No one can serve two masters. Either he will hate the one and love the other, or he will be devoted to the one and despise the other. You can not serve both God and money. (Matthew 6:24 NIV)

❦

You must love what God loves and hate what he hates from a sincere heart. You have to want to change the direction of your life. Crying does not mean that you want to change but is an emotion. The same people going to the altar Sunday after Sunday crying, but that does not mean that they are sorrowful for what they have done. There are some that are desperate for change and are crying out of a pure heart. You will know the ones that are desperate for a touch from the Master because you may see them in the next month or two and you may not recognize who they are. God has transformed their heart at the altar. We all need an altar experience where we meet God at the altar and he burns up jealousy, bitterness, unforgiving, covertness, fault finding, judgmental, manipulation, and pride. These are things that you may not be able to see visibly, but it hides in the heart. God wants to get to the root of the problem which is the very thing that is blocking you from attaining your full potential and causing you to miss the seasons and timings of God. There have got to be a time in your life that there is not just an altar at church that you come to and cry for restoration. Set up an altar in your heart, in your home, at your job, in your car and you will began to see victory. It means to relinquish to the possession of, or control of another; bring forth, free, liberate, save transfer, pass, remit, give or present. Liberate or free, loose, release.

When I shut up the heavens so that there is no rain, or command locusts to devour the land or send a plague among my people, if my people, who are called by my name, will humble themselves and pray and seek my face and turn from their wicked ways, then will I hear from heaven and will forgive their sins and will heal their land. (2 Chron 7:13-14 NIV)

The people of God would do good for a season then they would sin and God would have to chasten them. Then they would do good for a season and sin again and maybe receive another chastening. After a while God would allow the enemy to come against them and take them into captivity for a season. It was only for a season. There are some things in your life that you have done that have cause you to go into captivity. God never stopped loving them because they were in captivity, but he carefully watched over them day and night. He knew how long it would take for them to learn the lesson, and cry out for deliverance, so he placed an expiration date on their deliverance. God had it marked on his calendar that on a certain day, his people would go free. If you have fallen prey to the enemy, don't ever think that you are not coming out. There is an expiration date assigned to your deliverance. He's going to bring you out with a strong hand! For he is Jehovah Gibbor – The mighty man of war. It's important that you never forgot where he brought you from. Remembering keeps you humbly and in the right attitude of gratitude. God has always promised to restore you back to your original state, but restoration is always contingent upon what you do.

That's the covenant God has with you. If you do this, then I'll do that.

If the enemy has come against your finances, God wants to break the bondage. There may be lack in your finances because of something that you have done. Bad spending habits, not a good manager or steward of your money, or not tithing will eat up your finance. The Lord wants you to give the first tenth to him and it will be holy unto him which means the ninety percent that you keep will also be holy. You will see that you will always have more than enough. I do encourage you to take your bills and your paycheck and pray over them and offer them up to God as a sacrifice and he will give you directions on how to spend your money wisely. God can do more with the ten percent you give him, than you can with the ninety percent you have left. Try it and see don't it work. Trust him with your finances and he will rebuke the devourer for your sake.

If the enemy has come against your marital relationship, God wants to break the bondage. Maybe there have been a break in your marriage vow and the enemy is coming against your spouse and children because of something that you have done. Adultery and Pornography is now one of the number one secret sins that is plaguing our men today which is causing perversion and sexual misconduct even in the church. There are reported case after case of leaders in the church falling prey to the tactics of the enemy. God wants to deal with you in that area. It is only when you are open with God, that restoration comes.

There are many ways that God can chose to bring deliverance, but these four ways is how God delivered me you which is outside of the time and seasons of God,

1. Fasting and prayer

2. The anointing (consuming fire) will burn the devil out

3. Self-deliverance by the power of the Holy spirit illuminating sin

4. Assisted deliverance

I list these four things because they have been proven to work and you will find them very beneficial in your own life. There are some things that you can just pray about over and over and it still does not seem that you are gaining victory in that area. Fasting is like the gasoline that you put on the fire. When I think of fasting, I think of when the Israelite would make sacrifices to God on the altar and when God was pleased and the sacrifice was accepted, he would send the fire to consume it. There are some things that do not come out except, but by prayer and fasting. I suggest you begin a journal so that you can see God working. If you never expect Him to do anything you will never see it. I had been in church a long time and had never heard about fasting. Even after I got saved the church that I was attending never talked about fasting. The bible talked about "when you fast" that's how I knew that it is something that Lord expects you to do. The anointing helps you break free because there is a certain level of anointing that rest upon your life when you sanctify your life wholly unto to Lord. When you are follow his way through fellowship and obedience you become like a repellent, nothing can stay on your body. You will notice that things that you have struggled with for years, just seem to fall off. Self-deliverance is where the Holy Spirt will begin to point out certain things that are not like him. At that time, he is waiting for you to acknowledge that you agree and what he has pointed out is not pleasing. Repent from it and renounce it from a sincere heart and deliverance will come. You know better than your pastor what sins you are harboring in your heart, just deal with it. Assisted deliverance and where you can seek help from a pastor, spiritual leader at the ministry that can help you get free. Normally with this kind of deliverance you may want to write down everything that you can think of that happened in your family. It helps the deliverance.

If deliverance is the children's bread, why are still bound? why are you still struggling in certain areas of your life. Why are you letting words spoken over your life years ago still shaping your future? why are you not further along than you are? You have lack of commitment and lack of enthusiasm and drive. Bondage is from the enemy use to restrict or confine you. A limitation that is placed on you under legal or moral restraint or obligation. There are several reason people suffer bondage, either you don't know what deliverance is due to being misinformed or misguided. You may be bound because you don't want to face the reality that there is a real spiritual enemy that the bible so clearly speaks of that you cannot see that it is causing chaos in your life, and in the lives of others. You may be bound and not know it because you thought once you received Salvation, that you were delivered or perhaps when the subject comes up, you avoid it all together. Whether you acknowledge it or not, it does not make it untrue. The fact is there is an adversary because the bible speaks of it, and his job is to wear down the saints. Since we know that a spirit is a disembodiment it needs a body to operate. It could operate through a friend, a co-worker, a loved one, a child, a neighbor or even spouse. No one is exempt from being used. Are you in a church that encourage deliverance? Most Christians do not know that they need to be delivered. If you were to ask them, they would most likely ask you "delivered from what". There is a long list of things that we can start with that Paul was sharing with the Galatians. He was encouraging them that they were called to be free and not to been enslaved by their fleshy nature and desires because it causes bondage.

※

The acts of sinful nature are obvious: sexual immorality, impurity and debauchery; idolatry and Witcraft; hatred, discord, jealousy, fits of rage, selfish ambitions, dissensions, factions and envy, drunkenness, orgies and the like. I warn you, as I did before, that those who live like this will not inherit the kingdom of God. (Galatian 5:19-21 NIV)

※

You do not have the power to stop or to restrain yourself. It takes the power of the Holy Ghost to lose every shackle, chain, fetter, stock, noose and yoke so that you can walk in freedom. He is not just liberation, but he is our Liberator. He is not just Redemption, but he is our Redeemer.

CHAPTER SEVEN
The Journey of Faith

Looking through the eyes of God

Faith is journey, it's not something that you pick up when you need it and put down when you don't; like a spare tire that you keep in the trunk just in case you get a flat. What happens to the spare tire, if you never get a flat? It just sits there, unused. Most people never even check the spare tire to see if it is operable just in case they got a flat or blow out on the road. I head once of a person putting on a spare and finding out while driving that "the spare had a slow leak. God has set the fivefold ministry in the church to work collectively to equip the saints. Faith is trusting that God has it all figured out. All you need is faith to step outside of your reasoning and put the burden of responsibility back on God by holding God to his word. We have become so intellectually savvy that it limits our trust in God because we are always trying to figure it out. Faith is an action word which must be put into action because it is a journey and not just a word. That is one of the reasons the bible declares that faith without works is dead. If you truly believe something, you will respond with an action based on your belief. Whatever you believe, you trust in it. If you believe that God is sovereign, you will trust him and life in obedience to his word in every aspect of your life. What you believe will shape your life and your actions will be governed by what you believe. Faith is supernatural, but because you are created with a human body, you rely on your five senses to guide you, and that should not be. You allow the information you have gathered to shape the world in which you live, but it hinders our walk with Christ. You believe if you cannot see, hear, taste, smell or feel it, it does not exist, but the supernatural is outside of your natural senses.

I believe that God never intended us to be ruled or led by our natural senses. You were created to be led by the spirit within.

Now faith is being sure of what we hope for and certain of what we do not see. This is what the ancients were commended for. (Hebrew 11:1-1 NIV)

The book of Hebrew displays the wall of faith made up of the patriarchs who were commended for their faith. Everyone mentioned in Hebrew for their faith did something as a response to their belief. By faith God created the universe, He did not recreate something that already existed and he built upon that. When he spoke the universe into existence, He created it out of nothing. God used his faith when he saw how dark and void the universe was, he said let there be light, and there was light. Faith is the economy of the kingdom like money is the economy on the earth. We have all been given the measure of faith which is a proportion that is given to every believer. We are all given the same amount, but it is up to you to grow our faith. And how do you grow your faith, by simply believing the word of God. By faith Abraham, when called to go to a place he would later receive as his inheritance, obeyed and went even though he did not know where he was going, but he kept moving. Abraham waisted no time. I can see why he was called the father of Faith. I am sure that it was not easy for him to just pack up and leave his family and friends. You've got to get to a place that if God said it, you got to believe it and that settles it. How many times have the Holy Spirit prompted you to do something, but you sat still. Abraham did not stagger at the promises of God. His faith was unwavering as you can see through his actions. Abraham may have been reasoning in his mind like most of us when we are given instructions that are unfamiliar and have not been tried, but at the end of the day - Abraham believed God. Abraham undoubtedly had to face ridicule from his family and friends when it came to following God. It should not surprise you when people do not understand where God is calling you to go, and they may never understand. We all have a different assignment and there are some places that God may call you to that no one else can go, but you must be obedient to the call. You must live out your faith. My sister asked me once, how is it that I can believe God for certain things. She said that is amazing, how do you do that. I said "do what". She said "how do you believe God just like that. I said it is a choice. I look in the bible to see if God said it. If it is there, then I just believe him because he is not a man that he should lie.

When was the last time you believed God for something big? We serve a big God who does big things. I challenge you to stretch your faith. If you are barren, believe Him for a child. If you are single, believe him for a mate. Believe God for a new business adventure, A promotion, or Godly relationships and see won't he come through for you. God is faithful. Faith is like a muscle that must be exercised, start small and then you can graduate to something big.

Before I exercise my faith, I make sure that I am in alignment with his will otherwise it is not going to work. Then through scripture I make sure that it is the will of the father that I have it. It must line up with his word because God will not violate his word. Lastly be realistic with your expectations. Just so you can better understand and to give you an idea of what I am saying. If you are in need financially and you are praying to be rich, you may never see that happen for you. Why? God know the intent of the heart. If what you are using your faith for is to be consumed on lustful things that only satisfied you. There is a possibility that you will be praying for that a long time until your heart changes Our finances are to build the kingdom and to bless others. If that is not the intent of the heart, then don't pray to be rich. It only takes a mustard seed of faith to move your mountain.

Sometimes we make faith out to be some hard thing, when it really is not. I learned that faith comes through building a relationship. You put your faith in all kinds of things in your everyday life. If you work a regular job, you show up for work and you trust your employer that your paycheck is direct deposited in your account in two weeks. You never doubted this to happen. When you take your car to the mechanic, you trust that you find the issue and fix the problem. I like to call it misplaced faith because we can put our faith everywhere else except where it should be. Don't allow circumstance to shake your faith.

He replied, "Because you have so little faith. I tell you the truth, if you have faith as small as a mustard seed, you can say to this mountain, "Move from here to there" and it will move. Nothing will be impossible for you," (Matthew 17:20-21 NIV)

All things are possible to him who believe……….

Many of the people that received healing from Jesus was because of their faith. I have read scripture after scripture where he repeatedly said "your faith has made you whole". This walk is by faith and not by sight. To build your faith, you must hear the word. You can't hear anything else that takes away truth. Remember that there is a shield of faith that is part of your spiritual armor and it is there to refute anything that is not truth because it blocks every fiery dart from the enemy. Faith is a fruit of the spirit that is manifested as you begin to mature in Christ. You already have it, it is already in you. God will never tell you to use something that he has never given you.

CHAPTER EIGHT
The sacrifice of seeking

My desire is to know Him......

I want to know Christ and the power of his resurrection and the fellowship of sharing in his sufferings, becoming like him in his death. (Philippians 3:10 NIV)

Spiritually disciplining yourself is the sacrifice of seeking to know God at a greater level. Spiritual discipline is something to be worked on daily. You must consciously commit yourself to the work of the Holy Spirit allowing Christ to be formed in you. As a Christian you must spiritually discipline yourself just like an athlete before running a marathon, they discipline their mind and their body by putting it under subjection. By doing rigorous exercising, eating healthier, getting enough rest, drinking plenty of water. Spiritual discipline gives us a conscience awareness of the presence and power of God and helps us to draw closer.

I will share with you how I built depth in my walk with the Lord over the years which have brought me to a blessed place in him.

The Word

1. Set aside time to read the Word daily. If you are not a reader, and now you are a Christian you must discipline yourself to read the Bible. It is a slow process and your body will have to get used to it. Your body will be warring against your spirit to dominate in this area. For transformation to take place you must renew your mind until Christ is formed in you. Keep in mind that now you are born again, your spirit loves the things of God. Start small by setting aside some time every day at the same time just to read, even if it is only one scripture. As the weeks progress it will become easier to do. Before long, your Spirit within you will enjoy such fellowship with the Father, your spirit will be reminding you that it is time to read. As a "discipline learner", ask the Holy Spirit to give you some insight into the word of God. Ask him to take the small amount that you have read and show you how to apply it to your life. God is not concerned with quantity, but quality. What sense does it make to read a whole book in the bible for three hours and you cannot remember anything that you read. The Lord may give you just one verse of scripture

Trust in the Lord with all your heat and lean not on your own understanding; (Proverb 3:5)

It only took The Holy Spirit five minutes to speak that to your heart. You can take it and apply it to your children, your marriage, your job. No matter what situation you are facing, trust Him with all thine heart. The Word of God is the most tangible thing in all the earth because it is the expressed will of the Father to you. Read the word, then began to confess it over your life and keep confessing what you want to happen according to the word of God because God's word come with authority. When you began to declare it into the atmosphere, although you cannot see anything happening, it is changing the atmosphere supernaturally. The word of God will silence the enemy and it has the same effect on the lips of every believer when spoken. As you mature in Christ as a believer you must learn to walk in the word. It has nothing to do with how much you read, how many good deeds you do, how much you go to church. The question is: Are you putting into practice what you have read. The word of God is so powerful that the bible declares that the world was framed with it and is still being held in place by the word.

Look around you, what do you see happening in your life and in the lives of those around you. Are you experiencing a life of peace, if not find the root of the problem and began to declare the word of God over it? The Word of God cannot be broken, it is sure and will stand the test of test.

✦

Heaven and earth will pass away but my words will never pas away (Matthew 24:35 NIV)

✦

Everything in this life is uncertain and is rapidly fading away, but we have a calm reassurance that the word which was in the beginning will last until eternity because he is an eternal God, everlasting to everlasting. You can allow the very thing that God created to praise him, to keep you in bondage. Your mouth is a weapon against the enemy and when you allow things to occur around you that is contrary to the word and you not open your mouth and speak against it, it causes spiritual bondage. The word works and it will never lose its power because it is limitless and inexhaustible. It doesn't just work over some situations, but it works when applied to all situations because it is the word of the Lord. As a new believer, or even a mature believer you must speak about your conversion, confess the word over yourself, testify about His goodness. A lot of times you may not see the power of God working in your life because your confession has not become a reality. If I were to tell you that you are rich, but you never believed me, you will never tell anyone else about something that you do not believe. Every time you hear something on the television, radio or by word of mouth once you have reasoned in your mind that the information that you have obtained is true, you began to tell others about it. You are always willing to tell others about something that you believe to be true. If you are sick and the bible says by his strips you were healed, your healing will never manifest if you do not believe you are healed. It does not matter what your pastor said, how many people have prayed for you or over you. You must activate your faith and confess your healing by the words of your mouth.

❦

They overcame him by the blood of the Lamb and the word of their testimony; they did not love their lives so much as to shrink from death. (Revelation 12:11 NIV)

❦

You must believe the whole Bible, every word written by men inspired by the Holy Spirit which is for our learning. Take no thought to the opinions of others.

Everybody has an opinion of what they think, but what does the word of God say regarding that issue or dilemma. Everything that you may encounter while on this earth, there is an answer for it in the word of God, and unless you embrace the whole word, you will never live out your full potential. The word of God is like a treasure chest full of valuable items and there is an unlimited supply. If you are sick, there is healing in the word of God. During a crisis there is peace; there is strength for the weak and feeble.

⁂

As for God, his way s perfect; the word of the Lord is flawless. He is a shield for all who take refuge in hi. (Psalm 18:30 NIV)

⁂

You can read the word out loud, or you can listen to it while driving on CD or audio. Listening is beneficial because it helps you to remember scripture. Listening to the word strengthen your inner man which helps to build your faith. When the Holy Spirit remind you of a promise through a preacher or a pastor or another believer, your spirit will bear witness with the word which will also build your faith because the word comes to confirm what the Lord has already said. Discipline yourself to study to show yourself approved a workman unto God. Meditate on the word which means to ponder, muse, to focus one's thoughts. Biblical meditation is different that the meditation that we see going on in the world today. Yoga is popping up everywhere which Yoga is a Hindu spiritual discipline. Sometime you want to read inspirational books to inspire you and lift your spirit and make us feel good or better about yourself. There are books out there on how to increase your faith, twelve steps to freedom, how to accelerate your prayer life. As a Christian, all that sound good, but I was talking to the Holy Spirit about that one day and He reassured me that He is the teacher and it is Him alone that will reveal Jesus to me. He took me back to the first and most important commandment which is to love the Lord, your God. In other word, if I can fulfill the first commandment He will take care of the rest.

Prayer

Prayer is a necessity and should be the lifestyle of every believer because it is your life line for heavenly intervention. Some say that prayer is just talking to God, but I find it to me more than that. The disciples wanted to learn how to pray. They had seen Jesus pray so many times, he was always communing with his father in Heaven. Jesus being their example and yielding results began to stir up a desire that this was something that they should have been doing but was never taught. It was the disciples who after seeing Jesus pray so much, knew it was a life style so they went to him and asked him to teach them how to pray.

Prayer is one of the spiritual mandates in the life of every believer. There is nothing that can happened on earth without prayer because God will not violate his own law which tells you to ask. The bible makes it very clear it says "when you pray", not if you pray. Prayer is a spiritual weapon to be used against the enemy. Communication with the father is essential and prayer is something that we can do all day whether we realize it or not because there is a spirit within man that longs to commune with the creator. I can be walking through Walmart and although my mouth is not moving, I am praying in my mind to the Father. It is a privilege and an honor to be able to pray and have God intervene on your behalf. As a Christian if you are just starting out, you can pray this same prayer Jesus taught his disciples. Jesus is showing the disciples how to build a relation with the father through prayer. There are a lot of different ways you can pray. Standing, sitting, lying prostrate or even kneeling. It is not so much about the physical position, but the position of the heart.

⟡

This is how you should pray: "Our father in heaven, hallowed be your name, your kingdom come, your will be done on earth as it is in heaven. Give us today our daily bread. Forgive us our debts, as we forgive or debtors. And lead us not into temptation; but deliver us from the evil one. (Matthew 6:9-13 NIV)

⟡

Prayer is the vehicle we use on earth to take us into the heavenly courtroom of the Almighty God. Back in Jesus day there wasn't anyone to teach you principles like we have today. I remember when I first started praying, it was a struggle. I did not know what to say or how to say it. I felt awkward and thought it's not working. God took that little effort that I gave him and started to build on it. I started off praying the model prayer that Jesus taught his disciples, but as I grew in God my prayer language changed. I noticed the things that I read in the Word of God, I began to pray about them. My prayer life grew to be more fervent because I was believing what I was praying about. There is nothing in scripture that the disciples ever asked Jesus to teach them anything else except to pray. The disciples were mentored by Jesus for three and a half years and saw him walking on the water. They were in the boat when Jesus spoke to the storm. They were at the tomb of Lazarus when Jesus called him from the grave. They saw five thousand miraculously fed by two five and five loaves of bread. They saw Jesus healing and demons being cast out. They never asked Jesus to teach them how to fast, but they wanted to know how to pray. They saw Jesus always going away to a quiet place for hours even while they slept. Jesus spent more time in prayer and lest time healing. Prayer is essential, but we do just the opposite. The average person in prayer may spend twenty minutes but try to do accomplish seven hours of work that you have on the schedule. If we spend more time in prayer, it will take you a lot less time to do what is needed for the day because the Lord will give you wisdom. He will even let you know that there are some things on the list can wait until tomorrow. There were a lot of things that the disciple would face and Jesus knew that much prayer would be needed for them to overcome every obstacle, oppositions and persecution. Prayer is refreshing to your soul. It's like a cold glass of water on a hot summer day.

You can go to God with a burden and come out so light and carefree. Why? Because you were not meant to be burden down. You were not meant to carry a burden, that's why he said to cast them on him. Your mind is also engaged while praying that it causes your emotions to be very sensitive to the leading of the Holy Spirit and you will began to pray out His will on the earth. There are so many things that God wants to do on the earth, but we must pray that his king's dominion come to earth. The tactic of the enemy is to get you to stop praying by making you think that God is not listening or that you are not praying the right kind of praying. Prayer is a sincere desire of the heart that lines up with the will of God. Sincere prayer is what moves heaven and allows his kingdom to come from heaven to earth. Your prayer can allow or disallow anything that has already been allowed or disallowed in heaven, on earth in the name of Jesus. Make sure that your motive for praying is right otherwise you will be praying amiss. There is a wrong way to pray and dishonorable to God.

But when you pray, do not be like the hypocrites, for they love to pray standing in the synagogues and on the street corners to be seen by men. I tell you the truth, they have received their reward in full. When you pray, go into your room, close the door and pray to your Father, who is unseen. Then your Father, who sees what is done in secret will reward you. And like pagan, for they think they will be heard because of their many words (Matthew 6:5-7 NIV)

The Pharisees prayed in the market places just to be seen and heard by man. They had orchestrated prayer that was long and eloquent. Prayer had become an idol and very ritualistic and repetitions because they cared more about what people thought. When you go into your closet it can be a room in your house. A closet can also be a spiritual place where you go in your mind to close everything else out. A meeting place with God where to speak to him and you began to pray the mind of Christ which is prayer guided by the Holy Spirt. Jesus was not condemning them from praying in public and this is what most Christian struggle with. Most people are taught that prayer is private and individual and some tend to shy away from Corporate prayer for this very reason. Jesus prayed publicly along with Solomon when he prayed for the nation in front of the temple. You can set special time aside for prayer but it does not have to be at the exact same time every day. It would be very beneficial to start your day with prayer, it will set the tone for your whole day. In prayer you can exchange your mind for the mind of Christ and can give Him your whole day before you even get started. God graces us with wisdom in prayer along with strategies on how to handle certain situations you may face throughout the day. Growing up in the church we had prayer meeting every Tuesday night and I remember going as early and 10 years old and kneeling at the bench and staying on my knees for an hour or so and hearing the Saints pray to the Lord about some things that I did not even know that God was concerned about. Prayer is supernatural so the results will be supernatural. You will never be able to figure out how or what happens when you pray, but things change, situations change and most of all people change. Prayer is the vehicle that you use on earth that takes us into the throne room of God. No one can really teach you how to pray because it is not something that is learned. Prayer is birthed through the Holy Spirit. There is nothing that can teach you to prayer like a fiery trial! Some people don't pray until the trial come when we should be praying always. I remember getting up one morning for 5 am prayer. I would pray an hour before getting ready for work. I was praying one morning and asking the Lord to stir me up and make me fervent in prayer according to James 5:16 NIV which says "The prayer of a righteous man is powerful and effective"

Some of scriptures quote it differently because it talks about the fervent effectual prayer. I clearly heard the Holy Spirit say "I can send a trial to stir you up". While that may sound crazy to most people, I knew exactly what the Holy Spirit was saying. Think about it, some people never cry out to the Lord in desperation until something desperate or tragic happens, when there should always be a desperate cry in you to reach heaven and commune with the Father. When was the last time you cried out for someone's daughter like it was your daughter on drugs? When was the last time you prayed in desperation for someone to find employment, like it was your family out of a job? Most Christians are depleted and weary due to the lack of prayer or from being prayerless, but there is no excuse for not praying. It is a true saying: Much prayer, much power; Little prayer, little power.; No prayer, no power. This is something you should be doing, you should keep your own self stirred up in prayer. Don't wait until you get the call from the doctor about your condition. Don't wait until your school call about you about your child.

Your model prayer is to first acknowledge God and to esteem him and his attributes. Tell him *"You are creator of all things. Every good and perfect gift comes from you. You told the sun to shine and the moon where to go and hide. You are a good father who is compassionate, loving, kind and merciful. You are the creator of the universe"*. God wants you to tell him, not just think about it in your mind. Tell him he is all seeing and all knowing. He daily loads you with benefits. Tell him "you are the air I breath and if you would take my air how you would cease to exist". He wants to hear it from your mouth that apart from him, you can do nothing.

Tell him how weak and fragile you are and that you need him every second of the day, every minute, every hour.

The nation of Israel in the old testament had only known God as God, and not as a father so that thought he was a God of wrath. God was transitioning them to see him as a father. A natural father is head of the household, he is the one who hold the family together, and have the last say so in a matter. The father is the protector of the family and make sure all their needs are met. We should recognize that God is not on the same level as man, but he is our creator and not to be treated or approached as common. He is in Heaven and it is His kingdom not yours so you should pray that his king's dominion in heaven will be the same king's dominion on earth.

⁕

The seventh angel sounded his trumpet, and there were loud voices in heaven, which said. "The kingdom of the world has become the kingdom of our Lord and of his Christ, and he will reign for ever and ever." (Revelation 11:15 NIV)

⁕

Prayer is a place of transparency where you can be you in prayer because he already knows. You cannot make this spiritual journey in your own strength so prayer helps you to release the burdens and cares. Shame is removed in prayer and broken places are healed because of the peace of God. I have told God some things in prayer that I would not dare tell anybody else. Some things are just better said when you leave them in the presence of the Lord because he throws them away. Prayer is a real place that God deals with real issues. The Lord has something that he wants to do on the earth but he needs man to pray so that he can manifest it. Almost like Hannah, God gave her the desire for a child before she had Samuel although she may not have understood her desire to have a child was out of the burden of what God wanted to do on the earth. God knew the nation needed a judge, a prophet and a priest. I can remember praying over and over about the same thing because the burden was just that heavy. I bet every morning for at least two weeks or more when I got up for prayer, I would pray all sorts of prayers. It seems like I would get side tracked and start crying about this one issue I had that I wanted God to do. This was every day, but I did not realize I was doing that. While I was praying about it, The Holy Spirit said "Sing unto me a new song "I stopped praying because I thought to myself "that's strange, now what does that mean? New song, oh! Now I get it. A new song is something you have never heard before because it is new.

Holy Spirit was telling me to stop praying about this same old issue because he has already worked it out. He has moved on to the next thing while I am still stuck on the old thing. That's why you need to be led by the Spirit because he will teach you when to "pray until something happens" and when not to pray.

Hannah had to birth through prayer what God wanted to do on the earth, but once she got the word that God has heard her prayer, she stopped praying that prayer. Hannah was being tormented and made to feel that God wasn't listening, but she kept on praying until it manifested. Whatever situation you are facing now, His strength is made perfect in your weakness. Daily demands of life can cause you to feel overwhelmed and tend to pull your attention in every direction. It could be your job, your family, your business and it can cause natural fatigue as well as spiritually draining. If you are tired and weak, he will give you rest for your soul (your mind, will and emotions). We were not equipped to have to carry anything other than your cross. If you allow yourself to continually feel depleted, that is a good indication that you are not inviting the Holy spirit into your life and you are trying to face life alone. The lord wants us to live a liberated life, free of the cares of this world. Spending time with God grows out of a desire for him, a longing to know him.

Purge with Purpose and Emerge with Power

Cleanse me with hyssop, and I will be clean; wash me, and I will be whiter than snow. Let me hear joy and gladness; let the bones you have crushed rejoice. Hide your face from my sins and blot out all my iniquity. Create in me a pure heart, O God, and renew a steadfast spirit within me. Do not cast me from your presence or take your Holy Spirit from me. Restore to me the joy of your salvation and grant me a willing spirit, to sustain me. (Psalm 51:7-12 NIV)

This was the heart of David to always stand before God clean, with no hidden pretense. He always acknowledged his wrong and recognized it was always against God that he has sinned. This is the same word that King David used in Psalms 51 in his prayer to the Lord. Yes, your sin does affect others but it is first and foremost against God. The word *"Purge"* is found more than twenty times in the Bible and the meaning is simple. Purge means to 'take away to be clean', or 'to purify', or to *'cleanse'*. To get rid of, repeated emptying of the bowels. To remove toxins or excretion. Purging should be done prayerfully to see what area the Lord is calling you to. To deliver others you first need to be delivered, you must be the first partaker of the fruit. The entire Psalm 51 is a prayer of repentance to God from David because of the murder of Bathsheba's husband. David recognized first and foremost that yes, it was a crime that have hurt a lot of people. An innocent life was taken due to David's pleasure and satisfaction of having someone else's wife. But ultimately the crime was committed against God. Only God can forgive David and cleanse his heart. Purging is "inward". It is being led by the Holy Spirit to search your heart, the inward man. God knows the heart that is invisible to others, but it is visible to him and he sees the sin or iniquity that has separated you from him. If you are a believer, you can start by spending time with a pen and pad and being very intentional about what you are going to uncover. Pray and ask the Holy Spirit to show you your inner being, secret desires, hidden sin, things that you have been harboring that you pushed under the mat. The Holy Spirit will not only show you the things that you are doing that separate you from God, but he will also show you the things that you know to do, but you are not doing that has also separated you from God. Partial obedience is still disobedience which is as witchcraft. Iniquity is still sin but has to do with repeated immorality or wrong doings, it is a cycle. Ask the Holy Spirit to show you a tender spot, the wound that you have that has not healed. There is a wound in you that you keep covered up so no one knows it's there. Ask the Holy Spirit to show you the scar that left you wounded in battle, the arrow that pierced your soul and left you bitter. Your spiritual wounds are much like a natural wound. Wounds need time and air to heal properly. There are some natural wounds that even your physician will advise you "not to cover" because it will slow down the healing process.

Scars are left due to an injury by accident or surgery and your body's instinct is to heal and repair to wound. Sometimes marks are left on the skin or inside the body tissue because of the damage done. During my research, I found that the body produces something called collagen which is a fiber or tissue to mend the tissue broken by the injury which leaves a scar. Most people cover up scars because they are not pleasing to the eye to look at and mainly because visible scars raise questions from other. People always want to know what happened and how did you get that scar. How is it that your scar, now visible to others have become a conversation piece? Did you know most women who have had a child, because of the traumatic childbirth experience are always willing to share their story? I was talking with a lady who kept trying to tell me what happened when she had her first child. When I asked her how old her son is today, she said "oh, he's twenty-five years old and just got married". It has been more than twenty years and the pain is still in the forefront of her mind. The Holy Spirit through your purging wants to uncover your scar (s) in secret so it can be dealt with in private; to remove the shame and the pain because it is keeping you from fulfilling your destiny. Scars are destiny blockers and they keep you in seclusion and isolation because the enemy knows that someone else's deliverance is waging on you walking in total freedom and deliverance. So, we cover it so no one knows that it is there. David knew that un confessed sin was robbing him of his peace and joy and he felt the weight of the world on your shoulders. David's desire was to please the Lord, therefore he asked him to create in him a clean heart. The heart David had was wicked and David knew it. Did you catch what David said. He did not ask the Lord to mend or patch his heart. In other words, do not repair this heart, but I need a new heart. A new heart is heart that have never been created before because evidently the heart I already have is wicked and does not have the capacity in it to Love. Social media give suggestions on how to cover your scars, flaws and imperfections. We cover our wounds with permanent hair color, hair do's, cloths, make up, big houses and luxury cars. But on the inside, we are so broken. We were never given the time to heal. Did you know that the average person keeps a secret that no one else knows about? And sometimes take those secrets to the grave. You can use that secret to expose the enemy and set a whole generation free.

Purge Yourself

As the Holy Spirit began to illuminate certain things that are not pleasing to the Father, you will come to realize that there are certain things that the death of Jesus on the cross have given you the power and authority to purge yourself from. Purge yourself is what Apostle Paul was instructing and encouraging Timothy to do if he wanted to fulfill his calling in ministry.

cᵒᵉᵝᴺᵉᵗᵒ

In a wealthy home some utensils are made of gold and silver, and some are made of wood and clay. The expensive utensils are used for special occasions, and the cheap ones are for everyday use. If you keep yourself pure, you will be clean, and you will be ready for the master to use you for every good work. Run away from anything that stimulates youthful lusts. Instead, pursue righteous living, faithfulness, love, and peace. Enjoy the companionship of those who call on the Lord with pure hearts (2 Peter 2:20- 22 NIV)

cᵒᵉᵝᴺᵉᵗᵒ

If you were to look around your house you will see all types of cups, glasses and plates made from various things such as plastic, Styrofoam or maybe wooden. All these utensils were created for a specific purpose, but some are more valuable because of the condition of the utensil. If the president was coming for dinner, you would not serve him on a plastic plate. Most likely you would serve him on the good china which is something valuable and put out only for special occasions. You are a vessel created to be filled and used by the Holy Spirit. Purging yourself cleanses the vessel so that the oil or anointing can flow out. The purpose of a vessel is to hold something, but until it is filled, it is nothing more than an empty vessel. You are empty until the power of the Holy Spirit fills you. Once you are filled, it is only at that point that you can pour out to others. Paul encourages Timothy that he has been approved by God as a vessel of honor to preach and teach the gospel, to be a Glory carrier. Timothy's lifestyle reflects that very thing that he has received by faith because of sound doctrine that was committed to him by the power of the Holy Spirit. It is not enough to profess to be a Christian and go to church, but passively sit back and are not doing the work of the ministry mainly because your life is not set apart to be used by God. Your worth is not attributed to the vessel but to the treasure that is hidden in the vessel. Paul exhorted Timothy to remind them they should be striving to be a vessel of honor. Paul gave Timothy a picture of what a vessel of honor looks like when it is purged, compared to a vessel that has not been purged. It is always helpful when someone can illustrate the right way of doing something so that you can get the concept. If what you have been taught is done any other way, it would be considered wrong and the desired outcome would be different. You must be an active participant in working with the Holy Spirit to bring change so that you can be useful and not useless to the Master. You are the one who will have to crucify the old desires and nature of the old man. You will have to be the one who will have to break off those ungodly relationships. You will have to maybe even change professions or change friend. God is holding you responsible to change your outer appearance or dress. It is your responsibility to put a wedge between you and the world and anything that is unrighteous and displeasing to God. You must shun the very appearance of evil. It all starts with you. You must be willing and obedient if you want to be a vessel of honor, therefore you must make every effort to "pursue" (*search it out, be aggressive in looking for it, committed to finding*) righteousness, faith, love, peace with those who call on the name of the Lord out of a pure heart. It will never be found among those who only have a form of godliness but deny the power. Ask yourself the question: Am I honorable or dishonorable according to the statures of God. There are some things the Holy Spirit will not purge from you, you will have to willfully let them go. To be purified you will have to be the gatekeep and not allow the enemy to infiltrate and deposit garbage that will alter your course and prolong your season.

You will have to make a covenant with your eyes not to look at certain things on television or the Internet that grieves the Holy Spirit, defame or make mockery of the name of the Lord. Your eye is like a camera. Everything that you look at, once you blink your eyes now have a snapshot and it store these images in a file that you now have access to. The Philistine plucked out Samson's eyes. King Zedekiah sons were killed as he watched, then they plucked out his eyes before taking him to Babylonia.

It was customary that the enemy plucked out the eyes because they knew that last image that you saw, will always remain. It is now imbedded in your mind.

⚜

Your eye is like a lamp that provides light for your body. When your eye is healthy, your whole body is filled with light. But when your eye is unhealthy, your whole body is filled with darkness. And if the light you think you have is actually darkness, how deep that darkness is. (Matthew 6:22-23 NLT)

⚜

You will have to sanctify and put a guard over your ears from listening to certain music, audio teachings, negative speech, vain babbling, corrupt speech or conversation that is not pleasing to God that sows a seed of discord in your heart and causes an offense. Songs that use profanity or paint a negative picture about women or conjure up lustful thoughts are not of God. You will have to take the authority that is given you as a believer and take charge and sanctify your mouth to speak blessing and not curses. Let your conversation be pure and befitting. Let your tongue cleave to the roof of your mouth every time you want to speak something contrary to the word. I pray the Holy Ghost bridle your tongue because there is life and death in the power of the tongue. You will have to sanctify and cleanse the temple since now your body is a dwelling place of the Holy Spirit.

Make your temple a pure and Holy habitation. Do not defame your body by marking, piercing's and clothes that are alluring or provocative the draws attention to your body and not to God. Stop waiting on God to do all the work when he has already done it. We have first-hand knowledge regarding relationships and ungodly desires and attitudes. Anything in your life that does not bring God Glory and honor him needs to be purged. Confess your sins daily with an authentic desire to be more like Christ. It is a deception from the enemy if you think you have no sin. Hidden secrets will always keep you in bondage. You will be a prisoner to the memories, the pain, the hurt, the rejection and the shame which is the residue that was left behind. You must confess it, and you must take action.

The Holy Spirit will purge you

I remember when I totally surrendered my life to Christ, the Holy Spirit started the purging process. He woke me up one morning around three o'clock and had me to go through my house and remove everything that connected me to my old life. I went through every drawer, every closet, and cupboard. I was looking through all my movies, music collection, cloths, pictures and books. Anything that I found that did not bring glory to God I shredded them, packed it up in box and set it out for the trash. Holy Spirit will purge you, if you agree. It takes the Holy Spirit to show us how wretched we really are and that no good thing dwells in this flesh. After that time for at least the first two years I only read the bible. The word alone began to purge me, and the more I read the more liberated I became. The word of God revealed every dark place and exposed it to the light. Every time you read the word, you are being purged and ingesting truth on the inside of you which causes light to come in. This light is like no other light that has ever been shown. It goes into the inner most part of your being and it is transforming you supernaturally. No one can explain how it happens, but it does. You may have grown up without a father and it left scars of rejection. Maybe you have been abused by a relative and it caused abandonment issues. I grew up without a father, so I had a hard time receiving love from my heavenly father. I never really understood my biological father from a child and even now as an adult; I have just learned to love and respect him for who he is. On some occasions when I speak with him, he wants to go back to what happened in the past. I shared with him that the past is the past. I forgive him because now that I am saved I come to realized there were some things in life I did not do well, but God has forgiven me. The separation between my father and I, as I grew up caused a lot of indirect rejection and pain that most girls go through because of the father not being in the home. Looking back over my life it caused me to look for love in all the wrong places trying to replace that love with something else due to all the broken places in my life. I had to go through a season of healing. It was a long season......

There are things that happened in your life that you may or may not have had control over. He wants you free, and to let you know that you are loved. What God has started in you, he will finish. He will get glory out of your life, and when he does you shall come forth as pure gold. There is nothing on earth that can stop the work, not the devil, and not the trial because you are rooted and grounded in Christ, walk in Him.

CHAPTER NINE
Doing the Greater Work

Moving from useless to useful

I beg you to help Onesimus! He is like a son to me because I led him to Christ here in jail. Before this, he was useless to you, but now he is useful both to you and to me, (Philemon 1:10-11 CEV)

God is calling you to do greater, expand your borders, stretch out your faith. You cannot stay where you are when you serve a God of unlimited possibilities. God's desire is that his will, now become your will. Jesus called the disciples to himself so that he could teach them and then send them out to make disciples through mentorship. Elijah and Elisha are a good example of mentorship. Have you noticed throughout the Bible no one was left unto himself? John the Baptist was the forerunner for Jesus. Naomi did a wonderful and loving job mentoring Ruth. You should find a godly person in your church for mentorship but check them out first to make sure they are seeking the kingdom. When you are seeking the kingdom, you are searching to know the king and his dominion. Seeking to know him in purity of heart and what is his divine will for your life. When Jesus was teaching the disciples, he was calming their fears about daily provisions. It is a natural intuition to be concerned about eating and drinking and having clothes and shoes or maybe even housing. Apply this spiritual truth to your life daily as you seek first the kingdom, and its righteousness everything that you have need of will be taken care of because God know what you need. There is no way you can seek the Father and he not bless you.

You are a kingdom citizen and the host of heaven is backing you up. What opposition are you facing? The gospel talks about this new place that you are called to live in called the kingdom. You have to be taught how to live in the kingdom in order to develop the culture of the kingdom because it does not come naturally. You were a slave now you are a son or daughter to the king who owns everything. You must understand there is a king that rules, provide and protect his citizens. You are governed only by the king and not by other nation. God did not create man to be ruled by man, but for him to be the only authority in your life. The earth is the Lord's and the fullness thereof and all them that dwell therein. You are now born into a new kingly family which has its own morals and values regarding, how to live, how to speak, what to eat, or where to go and what is acceptable. You may struggle on this journey because you do not want to let go of the concepts of the old kingdom. You want to hold on to that old life because it is familiar to you rather than to embrace kingdom living. This new kind of living is different than most cultures because you may lose family, friends, jobs, and other possessions when you live in the kingdom because it is the king who sets the standards. The king wants your devotion to his kingship and the kingdom. You are probably wondering "what drastic changes" and how you will be able to adapt or make the transition. The Holy Spirit will help you. There is a remnant in the body of Christ that have such passion and fire in their preaching, teaching, and singing and they are operating in the spirit of excellence as a reflection of the kingdom. They evangelizing with such a hunger and thirst for souls. You on the other hand talk to your neighbor, car pool with a group of people going to work and have not mentioned anything that will lead them to believe that you are a Christian. One of the deadliest deceptions from the enemy is "You have time" and because of this it causes you to procrastinate and fall behind schedule. If you think for a moment that you are right where God wants you, you may need to go back to the altar because none of us are. There is always another place in God that you should be striving to attain. Most of the time the enemy will convince you that are good, even when you are not. You may think since God is in control of your life, He knows how it will turn out and there is nothing for you to do. It is time for you take responsibility for where you are on this journey. Are to moving toward greatness or settling for less. Sometime you can become so comfortable where you are that you miss the timing of God for your life. A journey is the general activity of moving from place to place much like your Christian life which is a journey, a long trip given to you by God that will help you to discover some spiritual truths about you, God, and the enemy along the way. Embrace the experiences as God begin to reveal himself to you along the way despite detours and distraction which may have altered your route. The object is to keep moving.

There are things in life that will keep you from moving forward

1. Blame Game show no accountability or responsibility. Blaming others for where you are on this path is being childish and a big hindrance to moving forward. Fleshly instinct is always to want to shift the blame to someone else is common because not wanting to take responsibility for your action was an inherited trait that was first seen in Adam. This should no longer be your character because you are the descendant of Abraham through faith. Jesus has reinstated the lease which now allows you to operate in integrity, humility, and trust- worthiness. The enemy

will always provide you with an excuse for not serving God in a greater capacity. For example: If you have experienced abandonment or rejection as a child which caused you to feel unloved by your parents and have caused insecurities which later led to emotional problems stemmed from being pushed aside, discarded, excluded or displaced. That can no longer be your excuse! You were nine years old when that happened and now you are thirty-nine. That same issue should not be holding you back. The book of Esther tells the story of a young Jewish woman who became the Queen of Persia.

Esther was not her real name, but her birth name was Hadassah and she was raised by her cousin Mordecai because she had neither mother or father. She never let what happened to her as a child hold her from being the queen. When the king chose Esther to be queen out of hundreds of beautiful women, the scripture does not say she made excuses why she should not be the queen. Esther was already predestined to be the queen before she was born, she just moved forward and accepted her place of prominence despite the tragedies she faced.

2. Impoverished mentality is basically a person who cannot see themselves doing anything outside of what has already been done; particularly by their ancestors. This is a spirit

of limitation which is a form of bondage that I like to call the grasshopper mentally. God created you with potential far above anything that you can even imagine, but there are steps to maximizing your potential. Knowing who you are in Christ is the first step. Do not become a victim of mistaken identity, acknowledge who you are in Christ.

But the men who had gone up with him said, "We are can't attack those people; they are stronger than we are. And they spread among the Israelites a bad report about the land they had explored. They said, "The land we explored devours those living in it. All the people we saw there are of great size. We saw the Nephilim there (the descendants of Anak come from the Nephilim). We seemed like grasshoppers our own eyes, and we looked the same to them. (Numbers 13:31-33 NIV)

The enemy's job is to keep you in derision hoping you never find out the truth about who you are. Brainwashing is when repeated pressure is used causing you to radically adopt someone else's beliefs. The enemy repeatedly feed you information about who you are not, and what you cannot accomplish until you began to repeat and believe what the enemy says about you and your destiny. You cannot live your life based on what the enemy said. In the book of Numbers, God had already promised them the land, all they had to do was "believe God". Identity theft is a malicious plague that is causing people a lot of unwanted time, energy and money to protect themselves against it. That is how the enemy works, he spends all his time getting into your mind, thought, and ultimately your actions. He convinces you that you are not strong, righteous, blessed, or walking in the favor of the Lord. The enemy slowly starts to diminish everything that God says you are and tries to replace it with something totally opposite because the enemy want to influence the way you live your life. They saw themselves small in their own eyes. They never talked to the Nephilim's, so how did they know that they were small in their eyes. They made an assumption based on how they saw themselves.

3. Fear is sent to paralyze you and to keep you from moving forward. This is usually the weapon of choice because the enemy he knows your destiny. The enemy know that if he does not stop you, you will do damage to his kingdom and more souls will come into the kingdom. Fear has nothing to do with the color of your skin, your nationality or age. Have you noticed before you came to the Lord, you had no shame and no fear in what you did for the god of this world (Satan). it caused you no shame to use profanity in public or to dress provocatively. You probably cursed at people in traffic if they cut you off or wanted to get over without putting on their blinker. You

took ink pens, paper, paint, postal stamps, tape, and all sorts of things home from the office with no conviction before you got saved. Now that the Lord have saved you, every time you get ready to do something for the kingdom, you get faint about to pass out. If someone ask you to give a welcome at church, you get shortness of breath when you stand up. This is a trick of the enemy to close your mouth and keep you bound. Can you now understand why there are so many people in the church sitting down, doing nothing? God has empowered you to do great things, to change the world around you, to impact your neighbors, and to influence the people on your job. Change the atmosphere at the post office, the grocery store, the gas station, the laundromat, the auto repair shop, the hair salon, the bank and even the gym. That's why when you get fearful, you should immediately recognize that's not the Holy Spirit and immediately bind it up!

❧

For God has not given us a spirit of fear, but of power, and of love and of a sound mind (2 Timothy 1:7 NKJV)

❧

When we align our lives with the will of the father we will see God kind of results. When we speak what the father speaks, do the work that the father is doing, then things will begin to manifest because the words that you speak are spirit and they are life. The words you speak have creative ability. The same authority that Jesus had in his mouth to cast out devils will be the same authority that your words will have when you speak. Anything that you encounter that is contrary to the will or the word of God, you have the power to bind it up and cast it out. Poverty is not your portion, sickness is not your inheritance, by faith you can lay hands on the sick and they shall recover. Did you catch that? the word says they shall recover. It is definite, end of the discussion. Jesus is the Word so as you began to declare his word you are declaring what he would be declaring because you are his mouth piece. The spirit of fear loves to dominate you by telling you what you can't do: I remember being fearful to speak in church, even just the thought of standing up made me nausea, my palms would sweat and my mouth would get so dry, but I have always wanted to say something about the Lord and how he has transformed my life. I use to look at other people and how bold they were and wished that was me. I remember as the Lord started to give me wisdom and revelation about his word, he developed a desire in me to want to share the gospel. I knew to share the gospel I would have to rid myself of fear. I realized that God did not give me the spirit of fear, so when the spirit of Fear would come to keep me from doing what God has said; I would pray and renounce it. There were a lot of people in the bible just like me fearful.

Do you remember the story in the bible when Elijah confronted King Ahab and slew the prophets of Baal? When Jezebel heard about it, she sent a death threat to Elijah and he became so fearful that he ran for his life and hid in a cave. But the word of the Lord said, "What are you doing here Elijah?" God knew how Elijah got there. That was a rhetorical question; God was not looking for an answer because God knows your potential. God knew that he had called Elijah as a prophet to stand during adversity and see his salvation. God wanted Elijah to know that there was no mistake when God called him. There will come a time you will face adversity. Trials and tribulations are not an option and, there is no way around it. Just because Elijah was afraid does not mean that God was going to bypass him and get someone else to do the job. Now, God will get someone else to help you. God told Elijah to go anoint Elisha as his successor. He told Moses to go and meet Aaron, he is coming to help you and he will be your mouth piece. The calling is irrevocable and God is calling you out of the cave. There is a cloud of witnesses in heaven that is cheering you on. Come out of yourself, it is time for you to shine. The whole world has been awaiting your arrival. Zion is calling you to a higher place of praise. Sometimes it takes God to remind you that he never calls you to do anything without equipping you to do it. Everything Elijah needed was already in him when God called him. Keep in mind that this is the same prophet that the bible said earnestly prayed and it did not rain for three and a half years, prayer again and it rained. This is the same Elijah that prayed a simple prayer and called down fire from heaven. All it took was just one word from the enemy and it shook the very core of his being and set him on a different course. What word has the enemy whispered to you that made you afraid. The Lord spoke a powerful word to me one day when I was talking to the Lord and asking the Holy Spirit how I can overcome fear. He said "Do it afraid". From that day until now, yes there are times that I am asked to speak. Preach and teach I am very nervous, but I am obedient because I refuse to be stuck. Plus, God loves it when you rely on his power because he shows up every time.

4. Spiritual Complacency is a quiet false security rooted in self-sufficiency which is pride. Complacent people in the church are not really concerned about spiritual things. They compare themselves to others rather than to Jesus and in their own eyes think that they are better off. You may not have started out that way, you use to have a heart after God. Somehow you let material wealth dull their senses. You forget the God is the source of everything and not your job. The scriptures make it very clear that it is only through him do we move, breath and have our being. He is the center and when our lives are not centered around him, everything will begin to deteriorate.

Marriages will fail, and business collapse. The church need revival because most people in the church are fine where they are. They never go the extra mile, they don't volunteer for anything. They are prayerless and powerless. They do not like to be told that they are off track because they do not like to be challenged to do more.

⊙↝⊰❀⊱↜⊙

He who heeds discipline shows the way of life, but whoever ignores correction leads others astray. (Proverb 1:17 NIV)

⊙↝⊰❀⊱↜⊙

Solomon talks a lot about correction because correction goes against our human nature. No one wants to be corrected. Everybody wants a pat on the back, to be told that they are doing a good job even when they are not. Your flesh which is the sinful nature of man loves to be praised and put on a pedestal. It should bother you if you are not bearing any fruit or maturing in the things of God. Years ago, they use to call it straddling the fence, but really there is no fence. You are either hot or cold, converted or unconverted. The bible calls it Luke warm because it is so easy to be pulled in either direction. This is a dangerous place to be because temptations and the ability to compromise is greater due to your vulnerability. Small compromise leads to greater compromise because it hinders the work in you. A little sin opens the door to greater sin and causes a slow separation from God and it won't be long before you will begin to lower your standards. When people use to tell dirty jokes around you, you would leave the room. Now you are the one telling the dirty jokes because you allowed commonality and friendship with the world to invade your space and reverence for God. That why Jesus was warning the disciples about the "leaven" which is yeast that start small. Be zealous for the things of God, passionate about what God is doing in your life and in the lives of others. Worship keeps you surrendered and yielded. Normally, if you can't lift your hands and worship God from a pure heart it is usually because there is something that have separated you from His presence. It is utterly impossible to Love God and not worship him. When your worship increase, sin decrease because during worship the Holy Spirit is chipping at some impurities and showing you the idols of your heart. You should never allow things to replace your devotion to God and cause you to lose your fire and burning desire to repent. Repentance and renunciation of idols that you have set up with your money, your house, your car, your marriage, your children, your education, your business, your ministry is necessary. Israel began to follow the cultures of the pagan people who did not acknowledge God as their god and they did every testable thing under the sun. God was always reminding them not to be like other nations making carving images and worshipping it. In the Western culture your job can be an idol. Anything that takes the place of God that you rely on and look to as a source of strength and power. We live in a society where everything is permissible and people are doing everything. Some have lost their way; most people are being deceived. They call right, wrong and wrong right. There is a way that seem right to a man, but the end is destruction. Our unrenewed mind will always come up with its own idea of what is right and wrong because pride loves to be on the throne on your heart.

⟳❧✿☙⟲

All things are lawful for me, but all things are not helpful. All things are lawful for me, but I will not be brought under the power of any. (1 Cor 6:12 NJKV)

⟳❧✿☙⟲

Do not become satisfied where you are. God created you with Purpose so that you can live a life of abundance on purpose. Drifting through life tells me that you know that you were created for so much more but are trying to discover what it is. I believe that people who are trying to find themselves are really on a quest to find God and the meaning of life because they know that there is so much more to life than what they are experiencing. On the day of judgment, I do not think God is going to ask you about how many degrees you earned or what college did you go to. He wants to know what you did with what he gave you. How have you increased what he gave you? God

158

wants our lives to be sold out to such a point that whatever He ask you to do that your answer will be yes, Lord. We find zeal to do everything else but fall short when it comes to the things of God and always want to give him second best. It shouldn't be that way when the God you serve gave everything that he had.

CHAPTER TEN
Spiritual Maturity

You should be growing

It's time to grow up! The United states have the largest Christian population in the world, although not everyone who confess to be a Christian is following the teaching of Christ. So, to ensure that Christians are growing we must make sure that the gospel is centered on the foundation of Christ and not on sociology or psychology. You should be doing what the bible says: praying and fasting, witnessing, laying hands on the sick, casting out demons, preach the gospel. Every one struggles in life, but struggle is necessary to move forward in the things of God because it makes you and then it molds you. Take an inventory and acknowledge you should be further along by now and experiencing the fullness of God. Once you take responsibility for your failures and rely on the Holy Spirit, he will help you through. The devil wants you to gradually slide back to the old lifestyle, but God is calling you forward. Serve God now, Lay hands on someone now! Deliver someone and set them now! Time is winding up and too precious to lose another moment. There is someone assigned to your life, your path will intersect with someone who is also on a journey, a quest to do great things. God is looking for you to tear down the deception of the kingdom of darkness by stripping the enemy of his power and taking his weapons. To move on to greater works, you must have a strong will, made up mind and determination. Don't ever doubt if your salvation is real because you don't feel anything. Your feelings will always lead you wrong because your feelings are sensual and has nothing to do with your spirituality. There is a lot to be done in the kingdom of God, but to do great works you will have to experience God at a deeper level. You may never look or feel saved, because the kingdom is spiritual, not natural. The kingdom does not come with observation which mean you cannot see it, but it is real because the kingdom is in you. Yes, the "kings-dominion" is inside of you. The Jewish people in Jesus day was looking for the Messiah to come and save them, but they were looking for him to come as a natural king in royalty and power to over throw the Roman government which was oppressive. They thought the Messiah would come dressed in fine raiment with a crown and a royal scepter, but Jesus was not comely to look at. He did not look like a king, and neither did he act like a king. Jesus came from a small village called Nazareth, but he was the one that the prophets and the Torah wrote about. So, my word to you is "You cannot wait for man to affirm or confirm your calling before you step out the boat and walk on water." You will never look the part, you will never be smart enough, you will never talk the part; according to man's standards.

So, it was, when they came that he looked at Eliab and said, "Surely the Lord's anointed is before Him! But the Lord said to Samuel, "Do not look at his appearance or at his physical stature, because I have refused him. For the Lord does not see as man sees, for man looks at the outward appearance, but the Lord looks at the heart." (1 Samuel 16:6-7 NKJV

As you are growing in grace and love, the new man will begin to manifest the word because the word has become personal to you. That's how you will know that you are saved. They will know you by your love one for another.

In this the children of God and the children of the devil are manifest: Whosoever does not practice righteousness is not of God, nor is he who does not love his brother. (1 John 3:10 NKJV)

Love is a powerful weapon against the enemy because he cannot love. The word love is used so loosely in our society, we love cloths and shoes. We say we love our pets, furniture and even use the same word to describe how much we love our jobs, houses and cars. In the same breath we say we love our sisters and brothers, but slander, backbite, lie and gossip about those we love. If you say that you are a Christian and have not love, that makes you a hypocrite because love is from God and everyone who love is born of God and know God. It is imperative that we have love for one another not just in the body of Christ, but also for the whole world. It is impossible to love God and not love people. If we are to be world changers we must walk in love. Before Christ came, the world knew not love. Your love is active, you are no longer just reading, but you are living it out and that is true transformation. We have enough sense knowledge, but there comes a time that you should apply what to have read, seen and heard about Jesus to your everyday life. The fruit being manifested is the evidence of obedience. Remember earlier I said obedience is the key. Before you gave your life to Christ, there were some behaviors and characteristic that you produced that were evil and vile. The works of your flesh simply means that you were a slave to sin and had no control over your thought, your will or your actions which has produced death. Fruit that grows on a tree is not something that the tree can even control because just like a natural tree, once a seed is planted, the natural circumstances of the earth will cause the fruit to automatically grow in its season. There are some fruit trees that bear fruit every year and some bear fruit every other year and some may not bear fruit at all, for several reason. If a tree is over fertilized, not pruned correctly and even frost bite caused by an early winter. Some trees may just stop producing fruit based on the age of the tree. Most people cover the branches or vines with plastic or some other material to keep the frost from getting to the root. You must prune a tree for it to bear more fruit. As the Holy Spirit began to prune things from your life, you will find that spiritual fruit will not all grow at the same time. It takes time and patience to grow fruit. There are so many kinds of fruits and each must be pruned differently. You cannot prune an apple tree like you prune a grape vine.

Prune means to trim or cut away dead or over grown branches, especially to increase fruitfulness. Anything in your life that keeps you from growing, increasing, living an abundant life. Anything that is dead, not productive which are things that cause stagnation, complacency will be pruned. Notice the difference, everything that this dead and unproductive that bears no fruit, he cuts off. Everything that bears fruit, he prunes so that it can bear more fruit. The fruit that is produce on the branch is only being produced because the vines is healthy. Connection is very important and vital to spiritual growth. Fruit cannot be produces on its own, it must remain in the vine. Apart from Christ we can do nothing, we are like a branch that is broken off and withered away. The nutrients of the branch are only in the vine. If you break off a branch and lay it next to the vine, it will die because it does not matter how close the branch is in close in proximity to the vine if it is not connected it will eventually die. That is how your life is, you must stay in relationship, close communion with God to flourish and blossom into a piece of fruit that is not just pleasing to the eye but is also delicious. The fruit that you produce should cause other to look at you in a different light. The world is a fruit inspector. They know authenticity of true love verses judgmental or hypocrisy. Christian are closely watched to see if you are who you say you are. If you claim to be an apple tree are you bearing apples? When you approach and apple tree, you should not have to wonder if what you see is really and apple. The fruit that is being produced in the life of a Christian is the characteristic of God, the father. You cannot be a disciple and not bear fruit. Jesus wanted to make sure that the disciple understood that you can tell what is in a man's heart by what type of lifestyle they live. False prophets were compared to wolves that disguise themselves as sheep. You can detect them by the way they act, just as you can identify a tree by its fruit. Did you know a healthy tree produces good fruit, and an unhealthy tree produces bad fruit? A good tree cannot produce bad fruit and a bad tree cannot produce good fruit. Yes, the way to identify a tree or a person is by the kind of fruit that is produced."

⁂

I am the true vine, and my Father is the vinedresser. Every branch in me that does not bear not fruit he takes away: and every branch that does bear fruit He prunes that it may bear more fruit. You are already clean because of the word which I have spoken to you. Abide in me, and I in you. As the branch cannot bear fruit of itself, unless it abides in the vine, neither can you, unless you abide in me. I am the vine and you are the branches, He who abide in me, and I in him, bears much fruit; for without me ye can do nothing. If anyone does not abide in me, he is cast out as a branch and is withered; and they gather them and throw them into the fire, and they are burned. If you abide in me and my words abide in you, you will ask what you desire, and it shall be done for you. (John 15:1-7 NKJV)

⁂

Spiritual maturity comes from spending intimate time with the Lord; it is more than going to conferences, seminars and church programs, it is more than that. It is simply living your life on purpose and allowing the Holy spirit to complete the good work that he has started in you. Spiritual growth does not come from reading the Bible although it can because reading the word of God is an invitation to know him. Keep in mind that having informational knowledge about a person does not equal a relationship. Normally when a seed is planted in the soil, the ground goes through all types of climates that is conducive to causing the seed to die so it can bring forth a tree that should bear fruit. The bible said that Jesus cursed the fig tree because it was producing figs which is what it should have been doing. It was a fig tree; therefore, it should be bringing forth figs. Like an apple tree that should bring forth apples. If you plant an apple tree, the tree will grow and there is nothing that you can do to keep it from producing apples? It will only produce apples and no other fruit can grow on that tree except what is in the seed. When the season come for the apple tree to blossom, it cannot be hidden. Prior to the tree producing apples, it is first a vine and then a tree. You should be growing and maturing in the things of God.

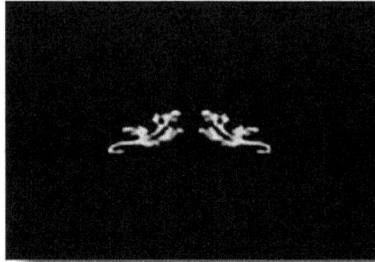

Just like the seasons change, so does life. In the next season of your life be like the tree in the autumn season that loses its leaves as it prepares for winter. Don't try to hold on to the leaves, let them go. You will not need them in the next season of your life

Dr. Carla Hunter

I pray that this book has been a blessing to you. I pray that the Holy Spirit spoke to your heart and reminded you of who you are in Christ and that you can do all things through Christ who strengthen you.

I pray that the favor of God overshadows you. I speak blessing upon your life. I pray that the river of Life flow to every dry place in your life. That the breath of God will breath on you and resurrect every dead thing and cause it to life again. I speak Life, In the matchless name of our Lord and Savior Jesus Christ.

About the Author

Carla Hunter is a Prophetic Bible and Seminary Teacher and Prolific Writer and Minister of the Gospel of Jesus Christ. Carla was consecrated and anointed into the office of an Elder by Chief Apostle Alvin McCullough and Sr. Pastor Jacque McCullough of Manna from Heaven Ministries International in Douglasville, GA.

She is a gift to the Body of Christ to preach and teach with simplicity. A native of Saint Louis, Missouri where she has lived most of my life until 2012 when the Lord transitioned her to Douglasville, Georgia to join her sister and her family.

She graduated from Southern Baptist Bible Institute and Seminary with a Bachelor in Theology (Th.B.). In January of 2016 she received a Master's in Theology (Th.M.) and June 2018 she received her Doctor of Theology (Th.D.)

She can be reached at carla@created4worship.com

www.ingramcontent.com/pod-product-compliance
Lightning Source LLC
Chambersburg PA
CBHW060751050426
42449CB00008B/1363